I'LL
STOP
TOMORROW

D0774407

I'LL
STOP
TOMORROW

Paul Campbell

MERCIER PRESS
WHAT YOU NEED TO READ

Mercier Press
Douglas Village, Cork
www.mercierpress.ie

Trade enquiries to CMD Distribution
55A Spruce Avenue, Stillorgan Industrial Park,
Blackrock, County Dublin

ISBN 978 1 85635 538 4

10 9 8 7 6 5 4 3 2

A CIP record for this title is available from the British Library

Mercier Press receives financial assistance from the Arts
Council/An Chomhairle Ealaíon

Printed and bound by Cox and Wyman Ltd, Reading, England.

CONTENTS

To Dee, a very special lady
without whose love and support
this book would never have been written.

ACKNOWLEDGEMENTS

Firstly, I need to acknowledge the people who were there for me at the end, when my world came crashing down around me. Tish, Dom, Pat & Gay, Pierce & Noreen, Geraldine, Jenny, and Sue, you should have run for the hills but you didn't – thank you. The man who first welcomed me into A.A. is now gone to a meeting in the heavens. 'J.R.' thank you for all the wisdom and understanding you gave me over innumerable cups of coffee in the Royal Marine Hotel. When JR left, the two Johns in Monkstown took his place, they kept my recovery moving forward at a difficult time in my life. To all my dear friends in 'Monkstown', a deep and loving thank you.

To Mary Feehan in Mercier Press who, to my amazement, liked what she saw in my first rambling draft of this book, you provided me with the motivation to complete it. To Clare and Miriam who made sense of my unreadable scratchings and never missed a deadline. Thanks to Barry, Nicola, Daryl and Keith for downloading emails, checking numbers and making sense of very scary computers. Thank you to those wonderful folk in the Open Door magazine who first asked me to write a weekly column and then encouraged me to get them published in book form. I would like to thank my lawyer Dylan Macaulay, who hasn't had to get me out of trouble in many years but who was, and is, always there for me. Finally, a big thank you to Bee Ring, a true friend, one who taught me so much about writing and addiction counselling, particularly the intervention process.

INTRODUCTION

Let me start off by telling you what this book is not. It is not a book written by an academic or a doctor. It doesn't have carefully drawn charts or squiggly diagrams describing a variety of personalities and behaviour patterns. I have read many of those books during my study as an addiction counsellor and although I learned a lot from them, I want this book to be different. It's going to be different, because it's written by someone who had everything and who lost everything; someone who went through the living hell of chronic alcoholism and the tough times of recovery. I want the book you have in your hands to help inspire your recovery, whether you are an alcoholic or the family of an alcoholic. I want to pass on to you everything I learned on my journey.

I'm a recovering alcoholic and I haven't needed to drink for quite a few years. Now, I write about my experiences with alcohol, my experiences in recovery, and the knowledge I have gained as an addiction counsellor. In my work as an addiction counsellor I'm still learning – learning about the complex world of alcoholism. I try to avoid theory because there are plenty of excellent books in that category. I want this to be an easy to read, a practical, hands-on type of book that anyone with an interest in the subject of alcoholism can understand.

During my drinking days I let down and hurt many wonderful people – my family and loved ones in particular. Alcoholism is known as the family illness and it truly is. Before alcoholism kills us it usually destroys the lives of our loved ones, the people who care about us most. Much of this book is written with these people in mind because the family is the silent victim of alcoholism.

Finally, readers of this book will notice what may appear to be some degree of repetition. This is intentional. If I return again and again to certain aspects of the illness (or co-dependency) it's so readers are continually reminded of the importance of the subject in question.

(N.B. Nobody can act or speak on behalf of Alcoholics Anonymous (AA). Any views or opinions expressed by me in this book do not therefore seek to represent that wonderful fellowship.)

Chapter 1

THE BEGINNING OF THE END

I awoke on Christmas morning alone. My pillow was sweat soaked and from every pore in my body came the sweet but rancid smell of stale alcohol. The physical pain from my pounding head was only matched in intensity by the agony of loss, self-hatred and overwhelming fear. But that morning there was a new sensation that even now I find hard to describe. I knew a quick but savage alcohol fix would relieve much of the pain but at the same time a faint yet persistent inner voice was saying to me, 'The game is up Campbell. Keep doing this and you're going to be totally and absolutely fucked'.

To those of you thinking I was merely overreacting to a thunderous, guilt-ridden hangover, allow me to put that morning in context. A year earlier I really had it all. I owned a highly successful advertising agency, lived in a beautiful home in an exclusive suburb of Dublin, and had a gorgeous partner who I loved (though not as much as alcohol, I was later to discover). I was wealthy, I had financial and emotional security and a circle of friends who enjoyed living life with the passion that I did.

Yes, I liked to drink but for a long time I didn't see that as a problem. I was in a stressful demanding industry – who didn't drink? For years I had been a larger than life personality. A therapist later told me that it was my crazy, passionate go-at-life attitude that helped me succeed in business and attract people to me.

Back to the sweat soaked pillow bit. Within the previous twelve-week period I had done twenty-eight days in the Priory Treatment Centre outside London, got sober, relapsed into drink again, lost my business, lost my partner, lost my home, lost many of my friends and, worst of all, lost myself. I hadn't seen it coming, but I had allowed alcohol to become the most important thing in my life. I chose booze ahead of everyone and everything. In the end it cost me everyone and everything.

Those were the thoughts that jangled around my alcohol-soaked mind that Christmas morning. As I lay there feeling that I hadn't a friend in the world other than booze, I knew I had a terrible decision to make -- was I going to live or was I going to die? I no longer feared death. What I could no longer face was the pain and fear of living as I did. The sense of shame, humiliation, self-loathing and the darkness of chronic alcoholism had led me to the edge of an abyss. I was sure the fires of hell, were awaiting me.

I had driven into Dublin on Christmas Eve to stock up on booze for the holiday period. The cacophony of festive music and brilliant colours only increased my sense of isolation. I stopped in at a pub to help kill the pain and talk my troubles through with my last remaining friend, Dr. Booze. After just one drink, a triple gin and tonic, I fled. The joy and happiness surrounding me was just too much. When I got back to where I lived (I couldn't bring myself to call it home), I unloaded a week's supply of booze. It was my intention to keep myself in drunken oblivion from Christmas to New Year and that night I achieved exactly that – a good lash of drunken oblivion. I remember waking up on the floor. I crawled into bed and continued drinking until I passed out again.

When I finally dragged myself out of bed on Christmas morning I knew I had to get out of the flat. I got into my car and drove. I ended up in Dun Laoghaire, in a car park overlooking the sea. Like an insane mantra I kept repeating, 'live or die, live or die?' I couldn't make a decision but the crashing waves against the sea wall looked so inviting. Five minutes, I thought, that's all it would take. I started up the car and drove off.

Whether it was the influence of some higher power or a subconscious urge for self-preservation I'll never know, but I ended up in Monkstown village a couple of miles from Dun Laoghaire. I had once been to an Alcoholics Anonymous meeting there and, as fate would have it, I saw a crowd flocking up the steps of the old stately building to the 11 a.m. meeting. Everyone in the room was dressed in their Christmas best, all except me. I hadn't washed or changed my clothes for days. The men and women at that AA group on that day all seemed so happy, so at peace with the world. I was offered a cup of tea, which I promptly spilled because my hands were shaking so much. At one point I came out of the defensive trance I had slipped into and it was as though I had left my body and was looking down on myself. I saw Paul Campbell, who until very recently was the Chairman of the board of Campbell Grey Advertising, but now he's a burnt out bum, a no-hope drunk. I hated what I saw. Suddenly I felt conscious of myself: my smell, my dishevelled clothes and my generally unkempt appearance. I quietly slipped out of the meeting and drove back to my flat along deserted streets, passing houses where glittering lights, warmth and love glowed through open curtains. I thought longingly of a very large gin and tonic followed by oblivion again, but for some reason, when I got back to the flat I fell asleep on the sofa before I got to the gin.

When I awoke it was dark and I felt strangely calm. For the first time in weeks I had no hangover on waking. I must have sat on the sofa for hours that Christmas night, lost in dreams of what was gone from my life and what lay ahead for me. My mind kept going back to the people in the AA meeting earlier in the day. The peace and contentment in that meeting was something I hadn't known for a very long time. I suddenly realised that I desperately wanted what they had. I had no idea how to go about getting it but even in my befuddled state of mind I knew that the key to it all was getting alcohol out of my life. Hours later I took a sleeping tablet and sought oblivion through sleep rather than booze. For the first time in months my sleep was free from nightmares.

I woke early on St. Stephen's day without a hangover.

What surprised me was that the sense of calm from the previous evening lingered. In a mad moment I decided to see if I could get through two days in a row sober (I told myself I could always go back on the booze the next day). I showered and shaved for the first time in four days. I managed to find some clean clothes, got dressed and headed out in the car for the 11 a.m. AA meeting in Monkstown. Halfway there I turned the car around. Who was I kidding? Sit through the meeting and then return to a flat empty of anyone other than booze? I got back 'home' and poured every bottle down the sink. As I watched bottle after bottle of gin go down the drain, I changed my 'live or die' mantra. 'God please help me, please help me', became a new and pressing mantra. For the first time in my life I admitted to myself that I needed help. I couldn't do this alone. I got back in the car and went to the AA meeting. As I sat listening to those wonderfully kind and caring people, I realised at long last that I was finally with people and in a place where I really belonged.

Alcoholism crept up on me, as it may have done, or is about to do, to you or yours. AA describes alcoholism as cunning, baffling and powerful. It's all of these and it can strike anyone at any time, young or old, male or female, religious or agnostic. If you have the illness then it does not mean you are an irresponsible, uncaring or bad person. Nobody sets out to become an alcoholic; indeed it's frequently passed down genetically. But if you have it, then it's your responsibility to do something about it. A wise therapist once said to me in a treatment centre, 'Paul when you're shaving, you are looking at the problem'. He was dead bloody right!

Those were crazy days when alcohol acted as high-octane jet-fuel to my system. In this chapter I hope to explain how it wasn't always so. Like so many alcoholics my progression to an unmanageable alcohol-fuelled life was quite slow and at times imperceptible.

My childhood wasn't anything out of the ordinary. It was not particularly happy, but I can't say it was all bad either. My father was a doctor and we moved around quite a bit, from England to Trinidad, back to England and finally to Roscommon. I was shipped off to boarding school at nine years of age. My folks, still living in England, were under pressure from my grandmother to ensure I got a good Irish Catholic education. I ended up boarding in Terenure College in Dublin for nine years. The first four years were like an extended nightmare for me, with lots of lonely nights and lots of bullying.

In those days any nine-year-old kid with an English accent was pretty certain to be jeered at every time he opened his mouth. Terenure was a big rugby school and I found that getting stuck into the game helped me to be accepted by the other kids. I don't want to overstate my unhappy time in boarding school because, truth be told, I actually enjoyed my last three years there.

It was in my last year that I took my first drink; I was eighteen. A group of us, on a day out from school, sneaked into a pub down on the docks. I drank a bottle of Phoenix Ale –I'll never forget it. I thought it harsh, rough and bitter. I didn't bother finishing it. So much for my initiation into the world of booze!

One might have thought that first experience of alcohol would put me off the damn stuff for life. It did put me off for a while, but like any alcoholic I discovered the benefit of alcohol was the effect, not the taste. After so many years in boarding school I entered the outside world with some trepidation. I found I was quite a poor mixer with strangers, and as for girls … I found those fragrant creatures scary (and still do). This shyness troubled me greatly until I discovered the magical shyness-busting power of alcohol. When I had just a few drinks (not Phoenix) my tongue miraculously unravelled, the fluorescent pink blushing disappeared and wonder of wonders, I could even manage something resembling a dance step. It would not be an exaggeration to say that I looked upon alcohol as a miracle drug. In those early days I didn't drink to get drunk, and I rarely did. I drank to relax my nerves and to move from the restricted world of chronic shyness to a place where I could live and conduct myself with confidence and a sense of freedom. Later in my life when working as an addiction counsellor I came to realise just how often alcoholism develops in those who use booze to conquer shyness. It becomes a very real social friend, an opener of doors and an imagined passport to a life without worry or fear. Unfortunately for many, at this stage, alcohol becomes their best friend just like it became mine.

I had managed to land a good job in advertising, as an account executive, while still quite young. My job involved taking briefs from the client, explaining those briefs to the agency creative people and then evaluating the advertising idea, before presenting and selling it back to the client. I was doing this with fairly senior clients in companies like Guinness and Boots when I was only twenty-three. Much of the client contact was done over an expensive lunch or dinner. In most cases there were copious amounts of fine wine, brandy and port involved. I soon realised that once we were all relaxing over a nice bottle or three, I was less intimidated by the fact that here was a twenty-three year old selling a deal worth thousands for a TV commercial to a senior marketing director.

I was good at my job. I was good with people – that is, providing you enjoyed a drink, at lunch, after work, or over a working dinner. I discovered that alcohol was a social and work lubricant. In those days it never hindered me. I had a good capacity for booze and I didn't get cranky or aggressive. I didn't throw up or pass out and I was cute enough to know when to stop, depending on who I was with.

Within a few years I was head-hunted by one of Dublin's top advertising agencies. Driving to work on my first day, my biggest concern was, 'What if these lot don't drink like the last lot?' I needn't have worried. The owner was the hugely talented and charismatic Peter Owens. Sadly, Peter passed away many years ago. Peter himself was not much of a drinker, in fact, I don't recall ever seeing him really drunk; he didn't like drunkenness. However, if you were good at your job, pulled in lots of business and didn't let the company down, he wouldn't object to serious wining and dining of clients. I soon found I was doing this every lunchtime and two or three times a week at dinner. I crossed the line when I began to go drinking with colleagues and friends on the nights I wasn't with clients. By now I had married a terrific woman, and I had two gorgeous daughters, Jenny and Sue and by the time they were seven and nine years old they saw me only at weekends. Over a period of about three years I had turned from being a warm, caring and fun husband and father, to one who was simply never there. What's more I'm sure they began to notice that I preferred work and drinking to being with them. In my mind, drinking vast amounts of booze was all part of the job. When the marriage eventually broke up, as a direct result of my drinking, my wife handled it with dignity and courage, which was a damn sight more than I did.

After my separation I went to work for one of the largest advertising agencies in the world. I was based in London, but constantly travelled for my job as international trouble-shooter. For at least three weeks out of any month I travelled to, or worked in, some far flung exotic destination, anywhere from Mexico to Sydney. My best friend Dr. Booze always travelled with me. I flew business class so I was able to enjoy the good wine and cocktails. By now I had a new relationship with a lovely woman back in Dublin and sometimes she came with me on trips to New York or South America. I was very successful and in a highly paid position, but I started to feel lonely for home. Most of my nights were spent alone in nice but sterile hotels around the world. With hindsight I believe it was at this point that alcohol really got its claws into me. However, my drinking never rendered me unable to function at work, even though my consumption levels were madly excessive. A typical night would be three or four drinks after a meeting, two bottles of wine over dinner, a couple of brandies and a nightcap in my hotel room. The smooth talking businessman would end up collapsed on his bed dishevelled and incoherent.

After a few years I returned to Dublin and started my own advertising agency. From the word go it was very successful. By now I was also living with my partner in a beautiful house in Ballsbridge. On paper I had it all. My business was thriving, I had a great team working for me, and my domestic life was now perfect. I had finally achieved everything I had ever aimed for in life. So what did I do? I got bored and I found, to my detriment, that when I'm bored I am at my most self-destructive. I started waking up with no memory of the night before. My behaviour would slip totally out of character. I would end up doing things that were bizarre and simply unacceptable. I started drinking in the morning, something I never ever believed I would do. I realised then, for the first time, I was totally addicted to the 'buzz', the 'hit' that booze delivered. Despite everything I had achieved I wasn't happy in my own skin and I used booze to numb my feelings and emotions.

There were rumblings of complaint from my staff and finally from my partner, so I started to visit a wonderful therapist, Regina. She was the first person to use the 'A' word. She told me I was an alcoholic and that I needed to stop drinking. But did I? No, all I really needed was a holiday. It was the stress that was the problem, stress, not booze.

For once things didn't go my way. After a series of ultimatums from everyone who cared about me (and I was rapidly running out of those) I ended up booking myself into the Priory Treatment Centre in London. I did it for no reason other than to get everyone off my back, buy time, regroup, get my act together and learn to handle my booze a bit better.

As long as I live I'll never forget my first morning in the Priory. Each day kicked off with a group discussion, ten of us sitting around in a circle. When I joined my first morning group, all my bravado and cockiness disappeared. As I walked toward them, I didn't see their faces, all I could see was a big box of tissues in the middle of the circle. Adults, sitting around a box of fucking tissues. Jesus. No way are the bastards going to make me cry. Adults weeping – Christ what have I let myself in for?

By the end of twenty-eight days I had done my share of crying and shouting and whispering and, for the first time in years, praying. The counsellors in the Priory were wonderful, very smart, but also warm and caring. The fact that they were all recovering alcoholics themselves helped us come to terms with the fact that we were too. But much of the healing that went on was within our own discussion group. We formed a close bond with each other, which helped us work through acceptance of our illness. Acceptance too that our lives had become unmanageable and had become so because of our drinking and distorted view of the world. 'Mental mismanagement' was an expression we came to hear and understand.

I flew home a month later determined never to drink again. I had learned so much about myself and the impact alcoholism was having on my life. I did stop drinking but that's all I did. I wouldn't go to AA or see my therapist regularly. I became a classic 'dry drunk': angry, edgy and resentful. After three months I drank again. It was the last straw for my partner. I had to leave our home, never to return. By now I had been forced to sell my business, so, in a very short period, my best friend Dr. Booze had cost me everything I valued in life. I continued drinking until that Christmas Day.

That all took place many years ago and since then I have found that by taking one day at a time, I haven't needed to touch alcohol. What's more, I don't need to today. I discovered though that giving up drink is only half the battle. Living and enjoying life without it is the real challenge. It took me a couple of years to get the kind of peace and contentment I yearned for but when it came, boy, it was worth it.

I'm living proof that there is hope for every crazy, out-of-control self-destructive alcoholic. I live in Kildare now where I work as an addiction counsellor. I'm good at what I do and it's not just because of my training and studies. I have a good success rate because of where I have come from. I understand the almost imperceptible slide from, 'a man who likes a jar', to becoming an alcoholic. I understand how our lives and those of our loved ones become so pain-filled and unmanageable. I easily identify with the despair, loneliness and confusion that clings to us as we slip deeper and deeper into denial of our problem.

Much of my work today is trying to help prevent those with alcohol/addiction problems from hitting the kind of catastrophic rock bottom that I hit. Put simply, I try to raise their potential rock bottom. If I have learned anything in this work, it's that there is no such thing as a hopeless case. I have seen miracles take place – men and women who have rebuilt lives torn asunder by alcoholism.

Some time ago I was asked to write a regular column on alcoholism for a magazine. The column covered various aspects of the illness from how to spot early danger signs to how best the family of an alcoholic can survive amidst the pain and chaos. These columns now form the basis of this book and chapter headings provide a guide to the content so, I suggest you dip in and out of the chapters that you feel you will find useful at any given time.

I hope, if you find your life being affected by alcohol or addiction that my thoughts and experiences will help you achieve what I have today – a nice life, full of peace and contentment. You can't ask for more.

Chapter 2

ARE YOU AN ALCOHOLIC?

I can't be an alcoholic because ...

I can't be an alcoholic because: I never drink at home; I never drink at lunchtime; I never drink in a pub (a housewives' favourite); I only drink pints; I only drink wine; I never drink on a Sunday (that was my line); I never drink in the morning; I never get nasty with drink; I can give it up for Lent. I could fill a book with various justifications as to why, despite chaos in their lives, some drinkers convince themselves that they don't have a problem. The fact is, for alcoholics, unprompted insight does not exist! For most alcoholics it's physically impossible to look at what drink is doing to their lives and decide to get help. Sadly, the vast majority of alcoholics only seek help when their lives hit a rock bottom e.g. losing their home, family or job as a result of alcohol. For some unfortunates, their rock bottom has to keep descending before they get the message and some never actually get it.

A lot of my work, and that of other therapists, is to use the pain of rock bottom creatively to help confront the drinker with reality and the consequences of their drinking. We hope to prevent an even more catastrophic rock bottom. When things start to fall apart for the drinker, they usually begin to make 'deals' with themselves and their spouses, e.g. they will only drink pints, or they will put two mixers in their vodka or they will only drink at weekends or after dinner or only drink wine, etc.

I tried making these kinds of bargains and they worked for a few days, sometimes even for a few weeks but the end result was always the same – a return to out-of-control destructive drinking. The harsh fact is that the alcoholic can never moderate their drinking. If they could they wouldn't be alcoholics.

The question I'm asked by families of alcoholics most often is –'Why don't they see what they are doing to themselves and the family and just stop drinking?' The simple answer is that they are in denial. But, as alcoholism is a complex illness, simple answers are never enough. Any illness that affects people physically, mentally and spiritually requires a recovery program that tackles all three of those aspects. One thing is certain – all alcoholics end up behaving in a destructive, anti-social manner, which usually hurts the family most of all.

Alcoholics feel badly about themselves. Their excessive drinking and behaviour while they are drinking fills them with guilt and shame. A sense of self-loathing becomes so strong they can't handle it, so they repress it. This is when real denial kicks in. Alcoholics often project their own self-loathing onto others, e.g. 'If you weren't such a nagging bloody wife/husband I wouldn't have to drink so much.' Alcoholics lose contact with their behaviour and emotions. They withdraw from their loved ones, physically and emotionally. Their defence system helps to protect them from what they fear and hate most – reality and responsibility for their own behaviour.

On a more positive note, I know from my own practice and from AA that there is always hope. A doctor in America was hospitalised sixteen times before he got sober. He then went on to found Alcoholics Anonymous!

The key requirements for recovery are:

- Acceptance that you have a problem.
- Acceptance that you need help and that you can't do it by yourself.
- Asking for help. Usually this comes by way of a treatment centre, AA, an addiction counsellor or a combination of these.

In my case, I tried to stop drinking my way, without asking for help. It didn't work and my drinking got worse! It was only when I felt totally beaten and without hope that I sank to my knees and begged God to do for me what I couldn't do for myself. Only then, and only one day at a time, did I manage to stop drinking (with the help of lots of AA meetings).

'If only' ... These two words feature prominently in the mind of the alcoholic who has hit rock bottom. For the fortunate few, the rock bottom may be no more than a threat from their employer or family, for others it could be disastrous – divorce or financial ruin. The ultimate rock bottom is death, and it's rarely a good or peaceful death, it is usually accompanied by shame, self-pity, self-loathing and despair.

Here are a few 'if only's' that will strike a chord if you or yours have a drink problem.

- If only – I learned from the pain that alcohol caused my family when I was growing up. How could I forget so easily the pain my father's/mother's drinking caused us all?
- If only – I didn't feel so comfortable with those heavy drinkers I used to hang out with.
- If only – I didn't enjoy the buzz of alcohol so much from the very start.
- If only – I got bad hangovers, maybe they would have stopped me drinking so much. (Interestingly many alcoholics feel 'seedy' the next day but do not suffer from horror hangovers.)
- If only – I'd realised what was happening to me when I lost my licence/crashed the car while drunk driving.
- If only – I slept better, then I wouldn't need a drink to get a good night's sleep. (Believe it or not this is a common rationale among alcoholics.)
- If only – my wife/husband wasn't such a nag, bully, wimp, etc., then I wouldn't need to drink so much.
- If only – I hadn't married so young/had married

someone else/had not got married at all.

- If only – I didn't have such a stressful job/terrible boss/demanding clients, etc.

- If only – I had had a happier childhood, then I wouldn't drink to kill the memories. (Yes, this could be true.)

- If only – I had listened and done something when people started telling me to get help for my drink problem.

- If only – I had asked for help when I started getting those frightening blackouts.

I usually try to point out that 'if only's' are not productive in any other way than to help people recognise where drink has brought them. This 'if only' way of thinking is likely to bring on self-pity, which is the last thing an alcoholic needs. Remember, it's never too late to stop drinking, embark on a recovery programme and get your life back. I've seen miracles happen in recovery and that's why I genuinely believe that there is no such thing as a hopeless case. If any of the above sets off alarm bells then don't let this be another if only. Ask for help!

Many years ago, my partner left me because of my alcoholic drinking. At the time I 'coped' by going on a week long bender. Later, I visited a therapist my partner and I used to see. I was in a bad way, sick from booze and brimming with self-pity. 'I've lost my best friend in the world,' I cried.

My therapist smiled gently and said, 'No Paul you haven't lost your best friend.'

Sensing hope I said, 'You mean she's going to take me back?'

In a kindly voice she said, 'Of course she's not taking you back, you're still drinking, aren't you?' I nodded. 'Well then,' she replied, 'you've still got your best friend haven't you? You chose alcohol ahead of your partner, despite her begging you for years to give it up. You chose alcohol ahead of her. Alcohol is the true love of your life!'

Boy did I go crazy at that comment, but in time I was able to see just how right she was.

Today, I regularly have to point out that same harsh truth: *If your drinking is causing pain and unhappiness to your loved ones and you continue drinking, then you love alcohol more than them. You're also an alcoholic.*

In a counselling session I will always communicate this sentiment early on. My own journey in recovery has taught me just how terrifying it is to hear the words, 'You're an alcoholic and you need to stop drinking'.

The message the alcoholic picks up is quite different; they hear, 'You need to banish your most trusted, loved, friend out of your life.' For the alcoholic, booze is the friend they seek out when they're happy or sad or angry or lonely or scared or just plain bored. In their mind, this so-called friend never lets them down, never fails to deliver the buzz they crave. Of course, these beliefs are all part of the illness called alcoholism. It's why AA so aptly refers to alcoholism as 'cunning, baffling and powerful'; it's all of those things and more. The only way for an alcoholic to get and stay sober is to make recovery their primary purpose in life. This can confuse my clients who say, 'But my sick father is the most important thing in my life' or, 'my children are the most important thing in my life'. Sorry folks, but it just ain't so. I've often heard it said that recovery, to a certain extent, must be a selfish programme and I agree.

It's a bit like the safety message before a plane takes off. The flight attendant tells us to put the oxygen mask on ourselves first – if we don't we may pass out and then be unable to help our children. It's the same with early recovery from alcoholism – if we don't put our recovery first we will drink again and then what use are we as fathers, mothers or children?

As a recovering alcoholic myself, I know how manipulative we can be. We can, if we are allowed to get away with it, always come up with what I call 'caring excuses' to duck and dodge various aspects of our recovery programme, e.g., 'I can't really give recovery my full attention until my mother comes out of hospital'. Oh yeah? Well the same mother would usually happily miss out on any number of hospital visits if it meant their child getting to their AA meetings.

A drink problem? Do the test and find out!

This questionnaire cannot on its own determine if someone is an alcoholic, but it can suggest there is a strong probability. It's called *The Michigan Screening Test*. It was first published by The American Journal of Psychiatry. If you are worried about your drinking or that of someone close to you, take the test and be as honest as you can. Count up your points to evaluate the score.

- Do you feel you are a normal drinker? *If no = 2 points*
- Have you ever woken up and not been able to remember part of evening? *If yes = 2 points*

- Does your spouse worry/complain about your drinking? *If yes = 2 points*
- Can you easily stop after 2 drinks? *If no = 1 point*
- Do you secretly feel bad about your drinking? *If yes = 2 points*
- Do you ever try to limit drinking to certain days/times? *If yes = 1 point*
- Do family/relatives annoy you when they complain about your drinking? *If yes = 2 points*
- Are you able to stop when you want to? *If no = 2 points*
- Have you ever got into a fight when drinking? *If yes = 1 point*
- Has your family/spouse gone for help about your drinking? *If yes = 2 points*
- Have you ever lost friends over your drinking? *If yes = 2 points*
- Ever got into trouble at work over your drinking? e.g. hangover, being late, ringing in sick. *If yes = 2 points*
- Have you ever drunk before noon? *If yes = 1 point*
- Have you ever had deliriums, tremors, severe shakes, heard voices, seen things that weren't there? *If yes = 5 points*

- Ever gone for help about your drinking? *If yes = 5 points*
- Ever been arrested drunk/drink driving? *If yes = 2 points*

How to score: 3 points or less you are considered a non-alcoholic; 4 points or more suggests you may have a problem; 5 points or more suggests you are probably alcoholic.

There are three levels of alcoholism – mild, moderate and chronic, and you can get a fair estimate as to where you stand depending on how high over five you scored. The important and frightening point is that alcoholism is a progressive illness, so if you enter the illness as mild but continue to drink, you will keep progressing until you become a chronic alcoholic.

I'm publishing this test because it's important that the alcoholic understands the nature of their illness from an intellectual point of view. Alcoholics need to do more than simply say, 'I feel bad about my drinking' because that's not enough. Unlike most forms of therapy, the alcoholic needs to apply thinking before feelings/emotions. It's a mental, physical and spiritual illness, therefore it's crucial that every part of the individual is treated simultaneously or relapse will usually follow. The saddest words I hear from some clients (usually after a few brief sessions) are, 'I'm grand now. I can handle it by myself'. These people just might stay off drink without help, but unless they work on the life issues that created the drinking behaviour they will never recover. I'm sure many of you know people who have stopped drinking but ended up cranky, angry, resentful and miserable. Successful treatment helps the recovering alcoholic learn to enjoy life without the need for alcohol as a crutch. I for one did not go through the pain of recovery only to be sober and miserable. I wanted to have a happy, peaceful and fulfilling life. Using the AA 12 Step Programme, and taking it one day at a time, I got the life I longed for.

If alcohol is causing a problem between you – you need to stop – if you can!

When a couple comes to me about the husband's drinking, the wife is usually hoping for a clear diagnosis. Is he or isn't he an alcoholic? Sometimes it's very obvious – at other times, like everything in therapy, it's a grey area. The one aspect usually present whether they are or are not alcoholics, is deeply entrenched denial. Let's keep this simple; if a drinker is allowing alcohol to come between him and his spouse then he has a real problem. If this has been going on for many years then it's a dangerous sign, really dangerous. If a drinker continues to drink, knowing by so doing he is causing fear and trauma for his wife, he's probably alcoholic.

Has his drinking crossed a line? Has there been instances of drink driving, shameful incidents or verbal abuse? In other words it's not just a wife with an anti-booze obsession, it is a real problem. Several times a month I hear new clients repeat the same mantra, 'I haven't got a problem, she has, it's all in her mind!' Once the sessions have reached this point I'm usually well on the way to a clear diagnosis. I always point out that even if they are now at the level of mild alcoholism, because it's a progressive illness, they'll end up a chronic alcoholic if they continue to drink.

Normal people faced with a distraught spouse who is threatening to leave would say, 'If alcohol is causing such a problem between us I'll stop right now'. Look at it this way, if eating apples made you cranky, behave badly and get into rows with your family, then you'd probably never touch an apple again. Makes perfect sense, eh? So, if booze has that effect on you, why keep drinking the damn stuff? You will keep drinking despite the problems it causes because you're alcoholic. Unfortunately, alcoholics are not able to live up to their promise to stop because they love booze too much to put any other relationship first.

Recently, however, I have come across a few cases that required me to reassess initial impressions. These cases concern wives who appear destructively alcoholic. In particular they are prone, when drinking, to clash aggressively with their husbands. In many cases, this occurs when the husband is a controlling, manipulative, self-centred bully and also usually a successful, aggressive businessman. What makes him good at his job makes him a lousy husband and father. He has often undermined his wife and, therefore, robbed her of her self-esteem and dignity.

What happens is that the wife bottles up and represses all her anger and frustration, but after a few drinks she develops the courage to snipe at him; after five drinks all her repressed anger and frustration burst forth in a totally understandable but unacceptable rage. The manipulative husband then starts telling friends, relatives, even their children, 'Your mother is an alcoholic, look at what I have to put up with'.

The truth is that sometimes she has become alcoholic, but often not. The real test is if she can she drink normally with people other than her husband? If she can drink normally sometimes then she may have an alcohol abuse problem, but there's a big difference between that and alcoholism. Either way she needs to ask for help!

Let us consider the person who knows they are in trouble but has not yet hit rock bottom. First, we must consider the words, 'knows they're in trouble'. If a person knows alcohol is causing trouble in their life and they continue to drink, they're probably alcoholic and because it's a progressive illness, it's almost certain they will end up a chronic alcoholic. Alcoholism never levels out, it always gets worse. *For the active alcoholic, unprompted insight does not exist.* No true alcoholic suddenly realises their drinking is out of control and decides to do something about it. Some may argue that even if the drinker has a vague idea of what's happening, they simply don't care. The point I'm making is that active alcoholics are incapable of seeing the chaos in their own lives; they are experts at deflecting blame and rationalising their way out of trouble. On a more optimistic note, many counsellors believe that out of crises comes the opportunity for recovery. By using a crisis, a counsellor can sometimes breach the wall of denial that the alcoholic has built around themselves.

Rock bottom is hard to define. What for one alcoholic could be a disastrous rock bottom, to another may be no more than a minor skirmish, e.g. drink driving. *What is common to all alcoholics is that for as long as they continue drinking, their lives and those of their loved ones will become more chaotic and unmanageable.* They will hit a series of deeper and deeper rock bottoms. A mere threat of divorce may work on some alcoholics, for others their spouse may have to flee before they seek help, and even then they may only sink deeper into alcoholic induced self pity and depression. Much of the work counsellors do is to try and raise the rock bottom for alcoholics. We try to help the alcoholic before they lose everything – spouse, children, home, employment.

There is, however, one situation that has a serious effect on the alcoholic's progress to recovery. I refer to the situation of a husband being forced to leave the family home because of his drinking. I call it 'black sack' day. We arrive home to find all our clothes and possessions in black sacks at the front door. It's usually brought about by years of appalling drinking behaviour where the alcoholic has clearly chosen alcohol ahead of his (or her) loved ones. What brings things to this point varies from couple to couple.

Strangely enough the 'final incident' is often something that to the outside world (and the husband) is quite trivial, e.g. an outburst of verbal abuse. I have worked with husbands after their sudden eviction and their response is often, 'How could she do this over something so small? All I did was roar at her. I've done that hundreds of times and she never reacted like this'. That's the picture from the husband's perspective, but talk to the wife and you will get a different picture. She will often recount a harrowing history of alcohol induced rage and temper tantrums; of how the family had to tiptoe around the alcoholic when they were drunk and also the next day when they were hungover. The alcoholic's attitude is to apply alcoholic logic to the situation; 'She's put up with me all these years, what's happened to change things now?' Let me drop in an observation here – women, I believe, tend to be considerably more tolerant than men, particularly around alcohol abuse.

Most men simply wouldn't tolerate their wives getting drunk several times a week; they'd be gone. Women put up with it for longer, but even the best of them have a breaking point. And yes, that point can be something small in comparison to the past unacceptable behaviour of the alcoholic. The line I hear from many wives afterwards is, 'It was the straw that broke the camel's back. I just couldn't handle it any more'.

The rock bottom that presents the greatest challenge is when the alcoholic has to get sober while living in much changed circumstances, e.g. alone in a flat or bedsit. Feelings of loneliness, despair, anger, hopelessness and resentment crowd every waking moment. Self-pity becomes a daily and nightly companion. The harsh reality is that this rock bottom, painful as it is, is possibly exactly what is needed to make the drinker take a long, hard and honest look at where their drinking has brought them. They have two choices – get help to change, or stay drinking and watch their life deteriorate even further.

AA, treatment centres and counsellors cannot get anyone sober unless they want sobriety more than anything else in the world. Getting a little sober is as unrealistic as being a little bit pregnant. While an alcoholic is drinking, they love alcohol more than they love their husband/wife/children. This is true because if it were not so then the alcoholic would stop drinking and prevent their family from suffering further pain. Let me again stress that alcoholics are not bad people. They suffer from a life-threatening illness and without help they can no more recover than a diabetic can ignore their daily blood sugar levels.

Chapter 3

WHY DO ALCOHOLICS DRINK?

I'm regularly asked why do alcoholics drink? One thing's for sure, they don't drink because they like the taste, they drink because they have to. Booze gradually slips into their lives and helps them cope with all the ups and downs of everyday living. In my work I often hear alcoholics express the view that they are just not happy in their own skin. Part of the reason alcoholics drink is because they're not happy or at peace with themselves. They drink to numb out uncomfortable feelings or the reality of life.

A couple of months ago a young man came to me for help. I still remember the fear in his eyes as he described the panic he would feel should he have to go out on a

Saturday night without getting drunk first. He described the gut-wrenching agony of trying to socialise with friends in a bar or club while sober. I believe that he'd have happily gone fifteen rounds with Mike Tyson in a boxing ring rather then get on a dance floor sober!

Unfortunately the poor lad thought that this was normal thinking. 'Sure all young people are out of their heads on Saturday night', was his view. Listen up parents: just because a great many kids are out of their heads at weekends doesn't mean it's normal or acceptable. It's not! Gone are the days when girls and boys needed a few drinks to chat each other up. Today they think they need to be blind drunk, stoned etc. It's this behaviour that causes A&E's to be packed full of mayhem at weekends. Recently I read an interesting statistic – in all recorded suicides over the last five years a total of 93 per cent had significant levels of alcohol in their body at the time of death.

To return to the topic of the fear of being sober in company/social functions, I well remember in my early days of recovery the gut-wrenching fear of having to go to a party, wedding or social event stone-cold sober. 'They'll all be buzzing with the booze in a few hours and I'll be looking at my sparkling water. No problem to them to dance around later, but me still sober, oh Christ'. I know it sounds a nightmare and for a while it is that, but I promise you it does get better, much better and quite quickly. As your sobriety strengthens you'll find that you can mix and talk without any problem or any booze. And no, you won't end up a bore, if anything you'll be more interesting and make more sense than the crowd at the bar. Of course there are downsides. I find even to this day that come midnight I tend to wilt a little. Even those not drunk get a buzz from a few drinks so they are able to keep going longer. I always have an agreed escape route if I know it is going to be a really late and loopy night. It's not that I am tempted to take a drink but I find myself getting a tad edgy around folk who have too much to drink and are starting to talk what sounds like Swahili to me.

Families of alcoholics frequently challenge the view that alcoholics hate themselves. 'There're so selfish they must love themselves', is a view I hear regularly. Yet at one-on-one sessions with alcoholics I often hear, 'I hate myself for what I'm doing to my family'. My heart goes out to both sides, but particularly to the alcoholic. They are usually wracked with guilt and fear. The fear comes because they can't figure out what is happening to them.

Where once they could control their drinking, now their drinking controls them.

Let me try and explain how this self-loathing takes hold in the mind of an active alcoholic. One day while drinking too much the person shows some form of strange behaviour, e.g. insults a friend's partner, gets into a fight etc. As they wake up with a throbbing hangover they think, 'I can't believe I did that'. This may be the first time they feel bad about their behaviour around alcohol. They may then start to develop excuses. 'I skipped lunch and drank on an empty stomach!' Then they decide that next time they need to have a proper meal before they drink so much. It never occurs to them that it's their excessive drinking that's the problem not the missing of meals. *Next to booze, rationalisation is the alcoholic's best friend.*

As their drinking increases their behaviour will, at times, become extreme. Now may be the time to finally ask for help. In the following weeks and months they will be regularly reminded of their increasingly out-of-control behaviour. In their mind they seem to spend a lot of time apologising for situations they can't even recall.

This downward emotional spiral becomes so painful they simply can't break free of it. At this time the alcoholic may visit their GP and say they are suffering from depression and often they are, but because they rarely own up to their drink problem, the doctor doesn't realise that they are in fact suffering from *alcoholic depression* and may unwittingly prescribe inappropriate medication. Now the combination of pain, fear and guilt is so powerful the only way to numb it is to hit the booze again. But this can, for the fortunate few, be the moment that they get a sudden insight into what is going on in their lives. It's the time they may just accept help.

Growing up with anger

I want to discuss an emotion found deep inside most alcoholics: anger. It's the fuel for much of what drives the illness of alcoholism/addiction. In many cases deep-seated anger was developed as a child within the family. For most people who they are today is a result of how they were nurtured as a child. A couple of questions to ponder:

- Were you loved as a child? Given hugs? Could your family express feelings?
- Was your home a strict authoritarian place? Harsh

discipline? *(Do as your told or else!)* Was there fear in your home?

- Did your father/mother treat their spouse badly, e.g. did you sometimes step in to protect your mother?
- Was there violence in your home by adults towards children?
- Did you regularly see alcohol being abused by your parents?
- When you finally left home, were you very glad to do so? Did you carry with you anger and resentment about what happened to you there during your childhood?

The above are just a few scenarios that can, and usually do, stay with us or reappear in later life.

Many of my clients will have fled home early in their teens to escape the physical and emotional violence. They get happily married and settle down. It's only years later that much of the repressed anger and resentment re-emerges. How is it dealt with? Often people drink to numb the painful memories. The repressed anger damages their new family, leaving everyone hurt and confused. I regularly listen to wives in particular say, 'I don't know why he's so angry, we have so much going for us at the moment'. The answer is that it's usually not about their current situation, it's often about unresolved issues from childhood. It's why many of us experience late onset alcoholism.

In my case, the issues of my childhood returned in adulthood. I developed a strange and confusing way of behaving and interacting with those around me. One side of me was loving, smart and very ambitious, the other, was quite self-destructive. Drink and other addictions fuelled my larger-than-life personality. I was looking for something, but what it was, I didn't know. I can't claim the usual cop out and say that I was looking for love because in early adulthood I met two wonderful women who really loved me, but in each case I allowed booze come between us. In each instance, my self-destructive personality kicked in.

Over the years two amazing therapists worked with me to help me understand the lonely scared and angry little boy that lived inside me. It was only when I managed rid myself of the need to consume mood-altering substances that I began to think and feel normal emotions, probably for the first time in my life. Today, I have a loving partner who doesn't know me as a drunk;

she's never seen me take a drink. I like to think I am a kind and caring person these days but don't get me wrong, I'm still a human being, capable of being a cranky bugger. Thankfully that just makes me like the rest of the people in my world.

Intolerance and self-righteousness – the badge of the alcoholic

The ball of anger that is buried deep inside the alcoholic can lead to intolerance and self-righteousness. The alcoholic can create a cocoon around themselves, which takes the shape of great charm and wit to the outside world but what about to the family? The kindest description of the alcoholic's behaviour towards their family would be 'difficult', but more a more realistic description would be 'impossible'. At work and at home they believe they are always right and any decision they don't agree with is wrong or stupid. Intolerance and self-righteousness are two of the more unpleasant characteristics of the addictive personality, but just below the surface, ready to explode, is anger. In truth the alcoholic is angrier at him/herself than anyone else. Deep down they are confused and scared about what's happening to them. They won't (or can't) admit that a person of their intelligence and strength of character has a serious problem with alcohol. They can't admit this because if they did so the next logical thing would be for them to do something about it. And that is a really scary prospect for any active alcoholic. It's why denial becomes a concrete wall around the addictive personality. In the mind of the alcoholic it's quite a simple concept, if they never admit to a drink problem then they never have to do anything about it.

Anger and frustration are very much part of the life of the spouse of the active alcoholic. AL-ANON does wonderful work in helping the family come to understand and accept that alcoholism is an illness and not an irresponsible weakness. The alcoholic never asked for or chose the illness. Put it this way, if your partner developed diabetes, you'd want them to get well again. But, like diabetes, the afflicted person must take responsibility for their own recovery. *If the partner takes responsibility for the alcoholic's recovery – the alcoholic won't!* Angry words usually follow – 'After all the help I've given you, you're still drinking.' Sometimes a relationship has to end before the active alcoholic finally accepts they need help. In my experience, however, most spouses will stay and support the alcoholic providing they see a serious and honest attempt at recovery. The proviso I put in here is that as a partner you should never settle for, 'I can do this by myself, I don't need help'. This never, ever works. Do not agree to it and put it bluntly to the drinker, it's the only hope of getting through to them. 'You've tried it your way so many times, now, if you want this relationship to survive I'm insisting you get help'.

I can stop whenever I want to

The word 'ego' is often used in a negative sense, but never by therapists. We are taught to understand that 'ego' is closely linked to a person's self-esteem. It's also a bridge between conscious and unconscious thought. All told, it's a very important word in any area of addiction.

To outsiders, the active alcoholic is gregarious, confident, even cocky. Those close to them, like the spouse, know differently. The alcoholic is often angry and depressed (alcohol induced depression), and deep down their self-esteem is very low. I don't want to overstate this, but many alcoholics just about manage to get by, to survive, by lying to themselves and others, cheating and engaging in self-destructive behaviour. This behaviour creates a wave of shame that regularly washes over the drinker. How do they handle this awful sense of betrayal of themselves, by themselves? How do they ease the shame and pain they have brought upon themselves? How do they numb the pain and fear? They hit the booze of course.

It's the ultimate destructive circle of doom. We feel bad about ourselves so we drink. When we drink we feel bad again. It all falls under the expression 'alcoholic logic'.

Is it any wonder then that in an occasional sober and reflective moment, the alcoholic asks, 'what on earth have I become? There is no hope for me. I am useless so what is the point in trying to stop?' In these circumstances you can understand how the self-esteem takes such a battering.

It is frequently after this reflective stage that serious denial sets in. The level of shame becomes so great that they simply can't cope with it. I have heard denial defined as the inability or unwillingness to accept the unacceptable truth. When the truth is so painful and frightening the addictive personality simply represses it, pushes it down into the subconscious. Addiction therapists witness this in practice daily. Several times a week I meet distraught spouses of alcoholics who tell stories of the appalling and unacceptable behaviour of the drinker. More often than not the drinker in question is highly intelligent and has a successful job. However, they can listen calmly to a tale of absolute chaos in the home, most of which has been caused by their out-of-control drinking and their usual response is, 'I don't have a problem, there is no problem – I can stop whenever I want to'.

This is an intelligent articulate individual speaking. They could talk intelligently on any subject but ask about their drinking problem and all logic and insight disappears. Their level of shame (usually well hidden) prevents them from acknowledging the full truth. One of the reasons alcoholics stay in denial, is that once they admit to their problem common sense dictates they do something about it. But then again, common sense is usually non-existent for the alcoholic in relation to booze!

Chapter 4

THE MIND OF AN ALCOHOLIC

'It's my football and if you don't play the game by my rules then I'm taking my ball and going home.' We've all heard children pulling this kind of stunt with their friends. For alcoholics, this attitude tends to persist in adult life. Life, and everyone in it, must at all times revolve around them. As the *Big Book of Alcoholics Anonymous* says, 'Self-centeredness is the root cause of all our problems.' If this sounds harsh on alcoholics, it's not intended to be. It's not that alcoholics are bad or weak people. They never asked to get this terrible illness and every active alcoholic would love to be rid of it. I say this as a disclaimer to fend off people who think I'm not understanding of alcoholics or that I'm unduly hard on alcoholics. Believe me I'm not. It's just I know from my own experience when booze controlled every aspect of my mind and soul that I wallowed in self-pity and pleaded for sympathy. Give an active alcoholic sympathy and you might as well hand them a drink. Sympathy in these circumstances is like putting an extra layer of cement on their wall of denial.

The greatest love in an active alcoholic's life is alcohol. After that they love themselves – but it's usually an intense love/hate relationship. Most alcoholics are incapable of offering unconditional love. Instead, their version of love tends to be, 'I'll love you, providing you love me back even more, care for me, mind me, forgive my drunken crazy behaviour, cover-up and lie for me and most of all never, ever criticise the love of my life – booze. This attitude is the reason active alcoholics often feel so threatened when their spouse attends AL-ANON. They wrongly believe that AL-ANON breaks up marriages and families. In their self-obsessed state alcoholics see anything that might lesson their control over their downtrodden spouse, as a threat. In reality AL-ANON has saved many a marriage, where without it, the spouse would have run for the hills years before.

There's a wonderful piece of AA literature titled

Just For Today. In it is the following suggestion; 'Do something, a good deed for someone each day …' Easy enough you might think? But for the alcoholic here's the difficult bit, '… and don't tell anyone you've done it'. Alcoholics are more than capable of great kindness but they tend to need to announce the fact to the world, which makes their motivation a tad suspect!

On a positive note, let me say that if an alcoholic works through a recovery programme and gets well, a new person will always emerge from the old. This person is usually kinder, wiser and very capable of rebuilding healthy relationships with loved ones. *Putting down the drink is not enough. Merely doing that usually creates a dry drunk: angry, resentful and more difficult to live with than when they were drinking.* Recovery is about getting honest with yourself – a tricky proposition for us all.

Meet Jasper – your addictive personality

There is an addictive personality that lives in the mind and body of the alcoholic. I always try to bring this to life by putting a name to the addictive personality. I call him Jasper and I for one know he can pop out, sit on your shoulder and whisper all kinds of addictive/alcohol logic into your ear. He knows us better than we know ourselves. This kind of addictive logic will make no sense whatsoever to a non-alcoholic.

You are, say, six weeks sober and you have struggled on a daily basis not to take a drink and gradually feel that you're making real progress. One Friday evening you're driving home and bang, it hits you: Jasper pops out and whispers in your ear, 'Look how well you've done, you've had a hard week, pull into that pub ahead and have a pint. You deserve it. You've proved to everyone you can give booze up, have a pint and start on the dry again on Monday. Who knows, maybe from now on you can actually manage your drinking. Go on, pull in and reward yourself with a nice cold beer'.

What happens? You have the beer and out pops Jasper again. 'Enjoyed that didn't you? Look, you might as well have another, be hung for a sheep as a lamb'.

At this point alcohol logic gets to work and you're back on the booze again. Next morning you may well ask yourself, 'What the hell came over me? Why was I so stupid?' In cases such as this, and there are many in early recovery, it's often down to subconscious complacency. Things start to go well in early recovery and unknown to ourselves we allow our early defensive barriers to slip. It will be difficult but in the early days we need to be constantly monitoring our thought process. We need to be constantly vigilant and recognising Jasper's addictive logic when we hear it.

Thankfully as part of a recovery programme we get to recognise his voice and his addictive logic in our head. The way to defeat Jasper is to be continually vigilant and continually monitor our own thinking and how we are relating to the world and people around us. If we don't, we eventually slip back into addictive thinking, which will then lead back to addictive behaviour. The good news is it does get easier with time.

My clients hate me saying it but when we drink excessively, alcohol is our best friend. It delivers that much needed hit or buzz every time. If in sobriety we do no more than simply stop drinking and don't take on a recovery programme, we discover that Jasper is not just a passing bad influence. Jasper and alcohol should be viewed as our worst enemy in life. Booze is never a friend to us, it always lets us down. Booze damages those closest to us, destroys families, careers and souls. What would we do with someone we once regarded as our best friend if we find out that they have been deliberately trying to destroy us and our family? We'd turn away from them, abhor them, banish them from our life. If we found out that this person had tried to destroy other people, we might meet up with them to talk about what happened and ensure that this evil person never got another opportunity to try and slip back into our life. That's exactly what AA is for. AA is about meeting people whose lives have also been blighted by alcohol, with everyone learning and gaining strength from each other's experience. If you have a problem with booze or can't stop, you need to recognise that it's your greatest enemy in life. *If it hasn't yet brought chaos and misery to your life and family then trust me, it will, and sooner rather than later! Be brave and get honest with yourself, today. Go and ask for help.*

The dangers lurking in the ordinary day

Today is not a great day, but then again it's not a bad day. It's a kind of ordinary day, the kind of day active alcoholics feel uncomfortable with. Alcoholics can relate better to great days or even bad days but they feel decidedly uncomfortable with anything 'ordinary'. They hate being bored or even worse, being seen as boring.

They need a regular whiff of danger which they perceive as excitement.

When alcohol and I partied together, we were always the hit of the party. I thought I was the witty, interesting, jovial, flirtatious one, the 'life and soul' of the party. In reality I was a drunk. I was boring, vulgar, obnoxious and frighteningly unpredictable. No better man to take you aside and tell you what's going wrong with your wife, life and family. But watch out for the raging self-righteousness should anyone offer a similar comment in return. Welcome to the world of the alcoholic!

It's the next morning, when our great pal Dr Booze has gone missing, that the scary bit kicks in: lying in bed, the pillow drenched in stale sweat, mouth tasting like mouldy copper coins and skin feeling itchy and dirty all over; getting out of bed pretending to be ok but the head feeling like it's just undergone botched brain surgery; those Saturday morning silent breakfasts; the quiet look of haunted despair from the spouse. They stay silent because what is there to say anymore? And you, you stay silent because you've run out of excuses. Truth be told, you don't really care anymore anyway. But buried deep inside you is your truth. What is it?

Take your pick: fear, self-loathing, resentment, self pity and bewilderment at what's happened to your life. Where is Dr Booze now? Some pal he turned out to be.

The above isn't over-dramatised fiction, it's part of my history, part of my journey through alcoholism. The memories of those days help keep me sober through these days. Believe me, nobody but an alcoholic has any idea of the fear, confusion and despair that inhabits the mind and soul of an out-of-control drinker. It's a very lonely place. That's the bad news.

The good news is that it doesn't have to be like this. *There is no such thing as a hopeless case.* In Ireland alone, thousands of alcoholics get and stay sober every year. They all share two things in common: they have a genuine desire to stop drinking and they have the courage to ask for help. I promise you, stop drinking one day at a time, start a recovery programme and you'll never need to experience this kind of morning-after atmosphere in your home. That's not to say we turn into saints, in my case not a chance! But the arguments and rows will be the same that every family faces. And at least you'll be able to remember exactly what you said the previous night and that does help, believe me.

Why the alcoholic always
needs to be in control

Many of those with addictive personalities share specific personality traits. For example, we tend to think in black and white. Alcoholics avoid grey areas – answers and decisions tend to be 'yes' or 'no', they are rarely 'maybe' or, 'I'll think about it' and definitely never, 'What do you think?' If we want something we want it now. If we do something we tend to do it to an extreme, or not at all. Even at work the functioning and recovering alcoholics tend to be overly fussy and worry about getting the job done to perfection. 'Good enough' is a rarely used expression for those with an addictive personality. *But above all, those with an addictive personality seek power and control.* The world in many ways is driven by power and control and it drives our daily lives. But, when control becomes a driving force in our lives, we can anticipate major problems. Eventually control becomes a bedfellow to manipulation. *Manipulation is usually the means by which alcoholics control those who surround them at work or home.* These traits create a false sense of power for alcoholics. Apart from being addicted to drink or drugs they also become addicted to symbols of power – material things like cars or houses. They can also become addicted to people – partners, girlfriends, etc. All these things can add to their inner sense of power and control. These unfortunates become addicted to the 'buzz' that control and power provide.

All of the above tends to create a false sense of self-confidence. The 'control buzz' tends to give them such a good feeling that they want to keep it going. It's not unlike the buzz they get from alcohol or drugs. Conversely, when these same folk feel they are not in control they become edgy. For many this is when they reach for a drink and try and numb the sense of low self-esteem.

In my work I see many alcoholics experiencing extreme swings between super confidence in some areas in their lives and extremely low self-esteem in others. Wives often comment that their high-flying, hard drinking, successful husbands can, at home, after a few drinks, turn into insecure and morose individuals. Questions such as, 'Is this as good as it gets?' are levelled at the bemused spouse and family. For the alcoholic personality nothing is quite good enough, no amount of success will satisfy them, particularly in their children's scholastic and sporting achievements.

These behaviour traits illustrate that for the alcoholic, putting down the drink just isn't enough. *A recovery programme has to address the dysfunctional thinking that has become a way of life for those with an addictive personality.* To be blunt, it's why some marriages break up early in recovery. Alcohol may no longer be in the drinker but all the 'isms' of alcoholism remain.

A 'functioning alcoholic' – no such thing!

A 'Functioning Alcoholic' is what I was diagnosed as many years ago. I believe the concept of a 'functioning alcoholic' is a contradiction in terms. In reality it's impossible to be an active alcoholic and still function as a healthy and caring human being. Alcoholism is a disease and the word disease means 'an involuntary disability'. Yes, one might, as I did for a time, run a successful business or hold down a responsible job, but if you look closer, you'll always find fear, pain and pending chaos in the personal/family life of the active alcoholic. Even today the memories of my functioning alcoholic years cause me pain. In many ways life was like trying to juggle red-hot coals, attempting to keep everything in the air but getting burned regularly. I could keep the business going, and even part of my social life was ok (if you call boozing with clients and my pals till midnight 'ok'), but lord, the stress of it all!

My life was made up of early morning meetings, trying to hide blood-shot eyes and mask the smell of stale alcohol with mouth wash and aftershave, chucking down painkillers to ease my pounding head, then making sure I 'lunched' with someone, anyone, who'd enjoy a few G&Ts, followed by a couple of bottles of wine. And later, trying to get through the afternoon at work before the buzz wore off. Ah yes, definitely a 'functioning alcoholic!'

I always had a few more drinks on the way home, during which I'd complain about how damn stressful all this business of socialising can be. (For 'socialising' read out-of-control drinking.) The stress at home was just as bad. It's always stressful trying to disguise a state of advanced inebriation, avoiding lengthy conversations, trying not to spill drinks, miss my mouth with food or fall over the furniture. The trick I usually used was to claim exhaustion or get to bed before my partner realised how hammered I actually was. (But of course she knew!) The saddest part of all this was that I had totally convinced myself that this was 'normal living'.

Today I ask myself, 'If that's how a 'functioning alcoholic' got through twenty-four hours – what kind of hell is it for a non-functioning alcoholic to get through the day?' The answer clearly is they are both the same. Alcohol is controlling them rather than them controlling alcohol. Their lives will rapidly become unmanageable. None of us can function properly when we abuse alcohol. It's interesting to note that for chronic alcoholics it's the marriage/family that usually goes first and only after that goes the job. It rightly demonstrates that most of the appalling behaviour around alcohol in the early days is confined to the family home.

Boundaries

When we see a couple or family who appear to have a good all round relationship we can be pretty sure there exists one particular behavioural pattern. They each, more than likely, respect the others' boundaries. The Oxford English Dictionary defines boundaries as: 'A line marking the limits of an area'. All of us have our own boundaries regardless of whether we are a six-year-old child or a sixty-six-year-old grandparent and our boundaries naturally change and evolve as our circumstances in life change. If as a child our boundaries were recognised and respected, then the odds are we will grow up well balanced and confident in our outlook on life.

In early adulthood we are often unsure of precisely where our boundaries lie, that is until someone crosses one. In some cases this can happen by accident, even carelessness. But often it happens through lack of respect by one individual for another. Respecting other people's boundaries is a wonderful attribute to carry with you through the journey of life.

Where am I heading with this? Let's apply the mind of the alcoholic to the subject in question. As we have said earlier, the alcoholic only sees the world through their own eyes. Their chronic self-centredness prevents them accurately seeing the world from another's perspective. Many textbooks state that alcoholics do not respect other people's boundaries. I would say it's not that alcoholics don't respect other people's boundaries, it's more that they rarely ever see another's boundaries. For example, a couple are separated and the father is an alcoholic. The couple's ten-year-old son lives with the mother and the father is due to pick up his son on Saturday at noon. By 1 p.m., there is no sign of dad. The son rings dad who says he'll be there in an hour. By 3 p.m. there is still no sign of the father. The son rings again.

'I'll be there in half an hour, stop being so damned impatient, I'm not going to forget you,' says dad.

Eventually dad turns up at 7:30 p.m. and then wonders why his son gets into the car so reluctantly and his ex-wife won't even talk to him.

What has happened here? The mother and son have both had their boundaries totally violated. She may have had her plans for the day ruined, and the son has wasted his entire day waiting for his father. If I had pointed out to the father that his behaviour demonstrated a lack of respect for his ex-wife and son, guess what his answer would probably have been? 'What are they complaining about? At least I turned up. Lots of separated fathers never bother to see their children at all, they're lucky I make the effort.'

I know for a fact that the father in question is not working through a recovery programme and is not going to AA. If he were he would be encouraged to change various aspects of his way of relating to those around him and the world in general. It would be suggested that he start thinking of other people's needs ahead of his own.

It's this kind of, 'working on yourself', that saves

relationships and marriages. As I have said before, putting down the drink by itself just isn't enough!

The 'deals' we make with booze

When a client first comes to me, I always start off by asking how I can help them. Often the answer is, 'I'd like to learn how to drink properly, in moderation'. I usually reply by talking about Audrey Kishline the founder of Moderation Management in the USA. Her book *Moderate Drinking: The New Option for Problem Drinkers* was all the rage some years ago. I can understand why. Wouldn't every 'problem drinker' just love to learn how to drink in moderation? The reality for Audrey was that while driving drunk over the limit she crashed her car into a father and daughter. They both died and she ended up in jail. Moderation is obviously not the answer.

I, and every other alcoholic on the planet, have at some point tried the moderation strategy. We cut down, avoid spirits, only drink at weekends, etc. Sometimes it works for a little while but it always ends up becoming out of control, destructive drinking. At the risk of slipping into shrink jargon, I suggest that 'moderation management' is a contradiction in terms. If one has to 'manage' ones 'moderation' then it's hardly moderation! Early on in therapy I usually ask two other questions:

- Can you accept that you have problems around alcohol?
- Can you accept that you need to do something about it?

This is called dual acceptance, and a 'yes' answer is needed to both before any real progress can be made. It doesn't mean that the client needs to stop drinking immediately (if only it were that easy) but it does require the drinker to accept the need for major changes in their life and around alcohol.

Recently a colleague of mine was running a group discussion among a group of prisoners in a British jail. He asked them, 'How many of you are inside for drink/drug related crimes?' Eight hands went up. Then he asked if they liked it in prison? There was a lot of growling at that. Finally, he asked, 'What's the first thing you're going to do when you get out?' The polite version of the answer was, 'get hammered', and 'get high'. I use this example to demonstrate the insanity of addiction. AA defines insanity as doing the same thing over and over again and yet somehow expecting a different end result. For the alcoholic who keeps drinking there's only one end result and it's a life filled with chaos, pain and shame, often followed by an early death. For the alcoholic who stops drinking and works on their recovery, the AA promise is a powerful one: a life beyond your wildest dreams. I know that to be true!

Chapter 5

WOMEN AND ALCOHOL

The majority of alcoholics are male but in recent years treatment centres and addiction counsellors report a significant upsurge in women of all ages seeking help. In my practice today almost 50 per cent of clients are women.

For many, it's a gradual slide into the world of problem drinking. It often starts with 'rewarding' themselves with a drink at six o'clock. Soon it becomes two or three drinks. Before they realise it they are 'sipping' throughout the afternoon. Finally it moves to a drink or two in the morning.

The unbearable stress of this double life and secret drinking only serves to drive the woman to 'numb out' the shame by drinking more.

In today's society a huge number of women work at least part time outside the home. Women regularly find that they need to do more than their male colleagues to gain the same recognition. Add to this the burden of also having to be mother and homemaker to both children and husband. It is no real wonder then, that many of them seek refuge from the stress of it all with alcohol – a few drinks 'to help unwind'. Balancing a career and home life, plus dealing with relationship problems is the perfect breeding ground for a potential alcohol problem. *Emotional problems appear to be a significant factor among women with alcohol dependency.*

In my opinion women get a pretty lousy deal when booze becomes a problem. Firstly, whether we like it or not, a woman having a drink problem is considered much more shameful than a man. Society appears to accept alcoholism in husbands/fathers but not in wives and mothers. Consequently, most women who show early signs of alcohol problems also have zero self-esteem and suffer terrible shame as a result of their drinking and their family's reaction to it.

Secondly, I believe that wives tend to be much more supportive of alcoholic husbands than husbands are of alcoholic wives. Many of my female clients get little genuine support at home as they struggle with the illness. Fortunately, the same women appear to possess real insight into what is happening to them and this helps them to respond well to treatment and a positive recovery programme.

Women need to remember that their health will genuinely suffer if they consume more than fourteen units of alcohol on a regular weekly basis. That's just two bottles of wine per week. And no, that does not mean you can run up the fourteen units over a night or two. They really should be spread over a minimum of four days.

I read with interest a piece in the *Sunday Independent* recently on the subject of the increase in alcoholism among women. Stephen Rowan, Director of the Rutland Treatment Centre, also commented that 50 per cent of the centres clients are now female. I believe that all of us who work in addiction counselling will have seen a similar trend. Rowan also identified a clear difference in the development of alcoholism between men and women. In many cases alcoholic men will have been abusing alcohol from as early as their teens. Women on the other hand tend to develop alcoholism later in life, often after their last child is born. Vodka used to be the main drink of women alcoholics but today it's usually wine. What starts as a glass with dinner on Saturday night, becomes a glass every night, becomes a bottle every night and, before long, a bottle during the day before the family comes home.

I regularily come across the, 'I only have a couple of glasses per night' line. Today's glasses, when full, can hold nearly a quarter bottle of wine. Two of these per night will have you drinking three times the recommended alcoholic unit per week.

Most of my female clients can, without difficulty, remember a time when alcohol simply did not play an important role in their lives. Not so men. In most cases men will acknowledge that booze was hugely important from as early as their teens. Alcoholic men can rarely recall a time when booze wasn't very important to them. This means that women with late onset alcoholism can harness many good and positive memories of a time when life was good and not dependent on alcohol. Women can harness the strength of their positive memories as part of their motivation to get sober. For male alcoholics, it's more difficult. They will have considerably fewer such memories.

I make a proviso here: the above refers in most cases to women over thirty-five years. Today, females of sixteen to thirty years old are, in many cases, indulging in suicidal binge drinking (six drinks or more in any one session). Interestingly, in Ireland today the various centres that deal with rape, report that only rarely do they actually find evidence of 'date-rape' drugs. Girls (and men) frequently report the next morning that their drink must have been spiked. Sadly, the reality is they simply drank themselves unconscious, thereby putting themselves in real danger. Please note, I am not implying that it in any way lessens the crime of sexual assault. The point I'm making is that drunk or sober we each have the responsibility to take sensible precautions regarding our safety.

Like young men, many girls don't drink to have a good time; they drink to get hammered out of their skulls. Many will start drinking heavily at home before going to the pub and then arrive at the pub drunk. These women will have few happy memories of a time when alcohol didn't feature largely in their adult life. Many of these young women will die young and die badly. How? Just read the papers any Monday morning.

Recent research indicates that Irish women are the heaviest consumers of alcohol in the world. The current trend amongst young female drinkers in particular is to match their male counterparts drink for drink. Ask them what the worst thing is that could happen as a result of this behaviour and you're likely to hear, 'The worst thing is we may get pissed a bit faster than the lads'. Unfortunately, that kind of thinking will lead directly to hundreds of early deaths amongst our female population. They'll die prematurely and often badly, covered in blood and vomit in their local A & E ward.

What few women realise is that their bodies react quite differently to alcohol than mens. It's not simply a matter of 'getting pissed faster'. An eighteen-year-old girl is not physically developed to the point she can handle alcohol the way a twenty-five-year-old man can. Remember, the booze these young girls knock back with such energy contains very much the same ingredients as antifreeze, and that's meant for the inside of motor engines! Many hospital consultants are now reporting serious life threatening organ damage among young women and most of it directly attributable to alcohol abuse.

Dr John Crowe, consultant in the Mater Hospital's liver disease unit, is one of Ireland's top authorities on liver damage amongst women. Dr Crowe recently pointed out that the female liver, when hit with cirrhosis, seriously impacts on life expectancy. A man with cirrhosis has a 75 per cent chance of being alive in five years time; a woman on the other hand has only a 25 per cent chance of still being alive in five years time. That's what I call a scary statistic. Dr Crowe also points out that a third of all heavy drinkers, male or female, end up with liver damage.

There is a physical and structural difference in how a woman's body reacts to alcohol. Our stomachs contain the enzyme, dehydroganase, which serves to break down the alcohol in our stomach and helps our body deal with the intruder. Guess what? Women have less of this enzyme than men do, which is the reason why women can't cope with booze the way most men can. I'll leave you with one last scary fact about the physical effect alcohol can have for women. In pregnant women, alcohol will cross the placental barrier so the unborn baby can suffer badly from excessive alcohol intake.

I'll risk making a forecast – I believe that in five years time women will outnumber men in most treatment centres. Sadly, the crazy out-of-control drinking patterns of this generation of young women will only be felt by society in the next five to ten years. The likes of the Mater will be treating the physical damage, while treatment centres and addiction counsellors will be trying to sort out the psychological chaos brought about by years of alcohol abuse. Along with all this, the maternity hospitals and abortion clinics will be dealing with the sexual consequences of, 'getting pissed a bit faster than the lads'.

Chapter 6

SOME PHYSICAL AND FINANCIAL CONSEQUENCES

What exactly is an alcoholic blackout?

By alcoholic blackout I don't mean 'passing out', I am referring to being unable to remember getting home or even large periods of a given night. This is called alcohol amnesia and is caused by part of the brain shutting down as a result of excessive intake of alcohol. Other than appearing to be rather drunk, the drinker in question appears to be able to talk and function quite normally. The blackout period can last minutes, even hours and the lost memory time never returns. (A drinker could knock down a group of school children in his car and never even remember it.) Blackouts are a strong indicator that there is an extremely serious drink problem present. Continued abuse of alcohol is likely to lead to long-term irreversible brain damage. AA members often refer to it as 'wet brain' syndrome.

Loss of memory is a symptom common to many alcoholics. It's also a very real problem for those around the alcoholic because it's difficult to cope with and understand. How often do we read in the newspapers of defence lawyers claiming, 'Your honour, my client had too much to drink at the time and has no memory of the crime of which he is now accused'? The suggestion here is that somehow if one is so drunk as to forget what happened, then one's guilt and responsibility are diminished. This nonsense continues to be used in litigation and sadly, it's clear that alcoholic logic is at work in law courts as well as in the mind of the alcoholic.

Let's bring this lost memory issue closer to home. A spouse is in the kitchen early one Saturday/Sunday morning and eventually the drinker emerges, hungover but chatting away none-the-less. The spouse looks on in angry disbelief and eventually says, 'Don't you remember what you did again last night?'

The drinker says, 'No, what are you going on about this time?'

The spouse replies, 'You promised not to get drunk again but you went for it big time and you ended up insulting our two best friends.'

Cue a blank look from the drinker. 'Honestly honey I don't remember it, I thought we had a great night.'

If a non-alcoholic began losing big chunks of their memory they'd hot foot it down to their GP. But an alcoholic begins to accept that these blackouts are par for the course for people, 'who like their jar'. Sure, it's frightening sometimes, but it's far too scary to discuss with someone who might suggest we have a drink problem!

The ability to recall shameful incidents around alcohol is also affected by repression. As the grip of alcohol tightens around them, the alcoholic starts to push down or repress memories of bad behaviour. They push it so far down it is literally pushed out of their minds. It's why getting honest with ourselves and taking responsibility for our behaviour is always the foundation for a recovery programme.

If reading this makes you feel uncomfortable, even angry or defensive about your drinking then you may well have a drink problem. If you do have a problem, then the sooner you do something about it the better for you and your family. By zapping out memories that are painful and deeply shameful we subconsciously create an environment that allows us to continue with such behaviour.

There are many serious physical consequences of alcoholism. Here is a list of some of them:

HEART: Alcohol is extremely toxic so can lead to weakening of heart muscles, resulting in heart attacks and strokes.

DT's: Delirium Tremors, leading to hallucinations. Alcoholics regularly die while having DT's.

BONE DISEASE: Increase in osteoporosis.

EYESIGHT: Home made poteen can blind.

PARANOIA: Very common but not often recognised for what it is.

IMMUNE SYSTEM: Heavy drinking affects the immune systems leading to chronic ill health, including liver problems.

CANCER: Alcohol abuse can cause a variety of cancers including tongue, mouth and intestines.

LIVER: Hepatitis is very common in alcoholics. Most serious however is cirrhosis. This is irreversible.

CENTRAL NERVOUS SYSTEM: Tingling in feet, legs

arms and hands? It could be peripheral neuritis. It is very painful and it could end up affecting physical co-ordination such as walking properly.

KARSAKOFF STATE: If your drinking brings on this condition you may well end up permanently in a mental hospital. It severely affects short-term memory, creates wild mood swings, incoherent babblings and bursts of violence. There is no cure for this.

SKIN: Broken veins on the face. Puffy eyelids. Psoriasis.

BRAIN DAMAGE: Often referred to as 'wet brain' syndrome. Large parts of the brain simply die off. Very serious permanent consequences follow.

HEARING VOICES: Alcoholics can start hearing voices. The voices can say foul and terrifying things to them. Naturally the alcoholic drinks even more to try and drive them away.

EARLY DEATH: Alcoholics tend to die earlier than the rest of the population. Choking on their own vomit, car crashes, falling down stairs, suicide. Hundreds of alcoholics die from episodes such as these every year.

So how much does booze really cost the family?

Like they do with most things in life, alcoholics tend to have a distorted view and attitude toward finance/money. These days booze isn't cheap, except for the 'happy hour' cocktails sold to young people in pubs and clubs (which in my opinion is the best example of social irresponsibility in society today).

In order to understand the financial implications of alcoholism it is easy to do some basic sums. For example, let's assume a drinker is spending €25 daily, six days a week, on alcohol. (This won't include the twenty times a year he/she might buy rounds of drinks for others and hangers-on who drink with them). If you add it all up, the expenditure on booze would be €150 per week, €600 per month and €7,200 per annum. Do this for five years and the expenditure on booze works out to be €36,000. All because of just €25 per night! This does not even include the casual use of taxis to get them home after a night on the tiles, or purchases of booze for home. In reality, for even a moderate alcoholic, we are probably talking about an alcohol fuelled bill of €10,000 per annum.

It's quite common for families where the principle

earner has a well-paid job, to still struggle financially. The male alcoholic often begrudges spending money on the upkeep of the home, a fact which can be seen by worn carpets, fading wallpaper and chipped furniture. Mind you, the TV will usually be wide, flat-screen and very expensive; it is his toy, 'his big soother!' Holidays will have been postponed through lack of cash, and the wife and kids clothing will mostly have been purchased in cheap department stores. But for the man it's usually a different story. 'I have to dress well for work,' is the usual line the spouse hears. And of course, 'I have to dress well on the golf course (and in the bar afterwards).' At Communion and Confirmation times the spouse of the drinker often takes up some extra job in order to pay for the basic necessities and then the alcoholic will arrive home with an over-the-top, 'get me out of trouble' present. The ever-suffering spouse will look on in horror as he presents a piece of glittering gold jewellery, when what she really wants is money for new school uniforms. Grandiose gestures are a real give-away trait of the alcoholic. In these difficult times the old bedfellows, shame and secrecy take up residence in the home. Lies and evasion become the currency of communication. Despair and bewilderment fill the spouse's waking hours.

The drinker meanwhile looks on as if nothing is going wrong. 'What problem? I don't see what's wrong with a man having a few drinks after a hard day's work?'

The good news is that this terrible cycle of pain can and does get broken regularly for both parties. If both parties have the courage to ask for and accept help, things often start to improve.

Chapter 7

CHANGING

It is a fact that at some stage alcohol starts to negatively affect every aspect of an alcoholic's life; loved ones, friends, finances, jobs and health. For these unfortunates there is no quick cure, but there is hope. Alcoholism is an illness and is frequently inherited. According to the World Health Organisation, alcoholsim is the third biggest killer after coronaries and cancer. *People can no more choose to avoid alcoholism than they can cancer.*

Nothing good can happen for the alcoholic until they accept they have a problem and are ready to do something about it. That's the first step in their recovery. Learning to live without the crutch of alcohol will be difficult. However, it is not just about their relationship with alcohol.

Recovery requires alcoholics to examine their relationship with themselves and then with others. Alcoholics need to embrace that dreaded word – change. I'm not advocating immediate and dramatic change (other than putting down the drink). I'm suggesting changing an alcoholic lifestyle for a new way of living. Primarily this involves a new way of relating to people. *Relationships are the first thing to crash around alcoholics but they are also the first things to improve and benefit from someone on a programme of recovery.* To stay sober we need to stay in recovery. To stay in recovery means ongoing change in how we relate to the world. It's demanding and in the early days, fairly tiring but I promise you it's worth it.

Over a couple of months the alcoholic will move from a life of chaotic drinking to one of ongoing recovery. During this period they will need to reprogramme every aspect of their lives. *Put simply, if you're an alcoholic trying to recover and you don't change fundamentally, then the old you will drink again.*

Why is the recovery programme so tiring? It is so tiring because the recovering alcoholic needs to scrutinise their every thought or action, big or small. The behaviour and thinking ingrained in the alcoholic from a lifetime of drinking will need to be continuously monitored. The kinds of things to look out for are any kind of excessive or powerful emotion such as resentments (the worst), anger, self pity, loneliness and mistrust. In my own early days of recovery I well remember being hypersensitive and ultra defensive about nearly everything and everyone.

On a practical level there are things people in recovery need to avoid like the plague:

- Regardless of how confident you feel, do not go into pubs/bars for a year.
- Try not to have alcohol in your home for six months.
- If you are having a dinner party, get rid of the booze immediately afterwards.
- Avoid heavy drinking friends and events.
- At social functions always have an escape route to leave early if you're feeling edgy.
- Take extra care if you're staying overnight in a hotel or on holidays. Avoid major life altering decisions for two years.
- Give yourself a fighting chance by going to AA or a treatment centre, or to see an addiction counsellor.

Recently I was asked what the best thing about being sober is. My answer is very clear. I wake up every morning and I usually feel good about myself. I'm not a saint by any means but these days I don't mess up other people's lives, or my own. I have a happy, calm and contented life, and so do those around me. Calm, would not be a word ever used to describe the home life of an active alcoholic. Calm and peace however, are to be found in most homes where an alcoholic is working on a recovery programme.

Strange as it may seem, fear is something that can help someone in an early counselling session. Fear is defined as an unwelcome emotion caused by the threat of danger, pain, loss or harm. It can also be linked to fear that something really unpleasant is about to happen. In other words, for the alcoholic, it may mean facing up to the consequences of their drinking.

It's one of those mysteries of the illness of alcoholism that those suffering from it find it so hard to accept the problems it's causing them and their loved ones. Sometimes therefore, fear can be a vital weapon in breaching a small crack in the elaborate wall of denial surrounding the alcoholic.

For the alcoholic facing up to the daunting task of getting sober, it's not just the thought of losing the family that creates such inner turmoil. It's often the thought of losing their best friend, Dr Booze, which creates most panic in the soul of the alcoholic. The thought of walking the winding road of life without the security blanket of booze is a terrifying thought in the early days of sobriety.

For the active alcoholic the buzz, the hit, which alcohol delivers is the most important thing in their life. They can survive days, even weeks, between drinking sessions secure in the knowledge that there is a good 'booze-blast' coming up.

Counsellors regularly hear people claim that they can go weeks without touching a drop so how can they be an alcoholic? My answer to that is always the same – it doesn't matter how much or how often you drink, if alcohol is causing problems in your life, particularly with your family, and you persist in drinking, then you are an alcoholic.

When I stopped drinking my biggest fear was that I'd become boring. I was scared that I'd clam up in company, have nothing of great interest to say to anyone and become a 'grey' person surrounded by sobriety. I've learned that it's the heavy drinkers who are the bores of society. Just listen in to any group of male or female drinkers after they have had a couple of hours of steady drinking. A bunch of demented witch doctors from Haiti would make more sense. No one really listens to each other in that company, everyone babbles away in louder and louder decibels.

When, the next day, 'euphoric recall' kicks in, drinkers can remember how they felt (or thought they felt) but frequently all details are blurred and jumbled up. In those alcohol fuelled sessions we rarely remember precisely what we said and did, but we remember that it all felt wonderful. 'Great crack last night, eh Jack?' We don't remember getting into a row with the barman, propositioning a friend's wife or generally making total fools of ourselves. We can't figure out how we seemed to have spent €200 on a night in the pub and a curry on the way home. We don't remember how we got the tear in our jacket or the puke stains on our shoes.

All this looks pretty dysfunctional on paper but in a bizarre way this is precisely what the alcoholic fears he is going to miss out on when he stops drinking.

As one who has been through it all, trust me, there is a wonderful and rewarding life for alcoholics who stop drinking!

Breaking through the wall of denial

It is important to insist on the alcoholic taking responsibility for their own recovery, but at some point you may have to decide to kick-start the process of getting them to face-up to the reality of their behaviour and mental mismanagment. By 'kickstart' I mean having an open and frank confrontation with the alcoholic. There is no need for drama, but be blunt. Tell the alcoholic to get honest with themselves and get help.

Be advised however, alcoholics hate the word reality, mainly because they are so rarely in touch with it. It's why a spouse usually finds it almost impossible to sit down and have a successful, 'can't you see what you're doing to yourself and us' type of conversation with the active alcoholic. The wall of denial they have built around themselves prevents them from absorbing these pleadings. The long-suffering spouse is often hit with indignant counter-claims that are laced with self-pity, e.g. 'There's nothing wrong with me – it's you lot who have the problem, anyone living with you would need to drink!'

Here are some suggestions and guidelines for a more structured intervention/confrontation between the family and the alcoholic.

- Catch the drinker off guard, ideally when hung over or just after 'an incident', but *never* when they're drunk.

- Have four or five 'persons of influence' present, e.g. wife, husband, mother, father, even an employer, but only if they are understanding and can remain calm.

- Rehearse what you are going to say, anticipate excuses and threats.

- Communicate that this is being done out of loving concern.

- Don't be judgmental. Avoid opinions like, 'I think you drink too much'.

- Be specific and blunt, e.g. 'You got sick and passed out at the office party'.

- Everyone present should contribute with an example of an 'incident'.

- Be prepared to be accused of disloyalty, etc.

- Hammer home that this is reality! Reality is not what they've been thinking it is.

The aim of this intervention is to break through the wall of their denial with enough reality so that, however grudgingly, the need for help is accepted by the alcoholic.

Do not accept vague promises to, 'cut down' or, 'get my act together'. Remind them that they have tried it their way before and it never worked. Be prepared for tears, tantrums, even a walk-out. Explain that despite how much you all love him/her, the family are no longer prepared to put up with the drinking and subsequent behaviour; it's simply no longer acceptable to any of you. Try and insist on a firm commitment to one or more of the following:

- Start attending AA meetings, minimum twice a week.
- Start seeing an alcohol counsellor.
- Enter a treatment centre.

Prior to an intervention, get everyone together and go through what each of you are going to say. If you have to, write it down. I can't stress enough just how manipulative the alcoholic can be. It's vital that the family keeps a strong united front and supports each other in the days following an intervention. If you get a commitment from the drinker then hound them to stick rigidly to it. Remember that out of crisis comes the opportunity for intervention and out of that, the opportunity for recovery. Even if the alcoholic storms out, you will still have achieved a lot. You may not have stopped their drinking, but I promise you, you'll have ruined it for some time to come and it may hasten their decision to ask for help. I know that my first glimpse of reality turned out to be the first step to recovery from alcoholism. (See chapter 13 for a more detailed review of the intervention process.)

Insight – we can't move forward without it

Active alcoholics tend to suffer from serious self-delusion. They genuinely can't see what they are doing to themselves and, more importantly, to others. *More than anything alcoholism is an illness of relationships.* The worst damage is often inflicted while sober – the lies, the blaming, the mood swings, the threats, the bizarre behaviour and the shutting down of emotional feelings. In short, it's the sheer unpredictability of living with an active alcoholic that creates such emotional turmoil for the family.

Years after I got sober my partner told me that what caused her greatest stress was not knowing which version of me would turn up in the evening – the happy drunk, the angry drunk or the sullen leave-me-alone drunk. The saddest part of all was that I didn't even need to be drunk to come home in those moods. *To add to the anguish of the spouse, the alcoholic usually manages to shift the blame, e.g. 'If you weren't such a nag, I wouldn't have to drink as much.'*

In recovery therapy, there are two early goals. The first is to reduce, and eventually eliminate self-delusion and the second is to develop insight. Frequently the alcoholic has no idea what their behaviour is doing to their family. The root cause of the problem is that alcohol has numbed their ability to experience genuine feelings (except anger and self pity). Early on in therapy, counsellors work with the alcoholic to help them get in touch with their feelings. Until that happens the recovering alcoholic has little hope of understanding the feelings of others. Gradually, providing they work on their recovery, genuine insight will come to them. They will begin to recognise their own and other people's feelings. This development of insight can be quite distressing but stick with it because it's an important part of the recovery process.

Having developed an understanding of their own and others' feelings, the recovering alcoholic will need to use this new found knowledge to change their behaviour, particularly around relationships. *Understanding how and why we have hurt our family is of little benefit unless we accept we also need to change our behaviour.* The alcoholic needs to learn how to relate appropriately to our loved ones.

It's an established fact that if the alcoholic doesn't change in recovery the alcoholic will drink again. They'll stay off alcohol for a while but will become angry, resentful and unhappy. In time they'll end up drinking to numb these feelings and the whole chaotic cycle will start again.

Don't fight it – surrender to the process

The topic for this section might be a touch sensitive for some. I want to write about what is referred to in AA as our 'higher power' or 'God as we understand him'.

I do not believe that one must believe in God to get sober – there is many an agnostic in AA – but in my experience it helps recovery in the early days if the person suffering from alcoholism has some belief in a 'higher power' or a God.

The words that always worry me when I meet a client in early recovery are, 'I can do this by myself. I have very strong willpower'. I gently point out that willpower has nothing whatsoever to do with recovery. If willpower worked the alcoholic would hardly be in the trouble they're in, would they? Strange as it may seem, it's surrender to the illness and to the process that is the key to recovery. Acceptance of our reality then follows.

My faith in my God is based on logic, which I know probably sounds a tad strange but there is absolutely no other explanation for some of the miracles that have happened to me in recovery. At the end of my drinking when I had no one or no place to turn to I asked God for help. God in return gave me renewed strength and purpose in my life. He gave me the strength to sit in a room full of strangers and tell them I was an alcoholic and needed help. Good things started to happen around me, things which at times defied logic. I believe that there is a power out there that works for good in so many ways. I don't believe that it's just the power of nature that makes the leaves turn green in spring or the sun rise gloriously every morning. I genuinely believe that the power that makes those things happen is a benevolent and caring God. Please don't misunderstand me though, I'm not a God 'freak' and I would never impose my views on clients or fellow members of AA.

There is often an interesting phenomenon that takes place in AA for those in early recovery. It applies to agnostics, people who believe in no God whatsoever.

What AA suggests to them is to accept that their 'higher power' could be the power of the fellowship of AA. Anyone who has been at an AA meeting can confirm that this power exists in the room when a group of alcoholics gather to lend support to each other. The concept itself is usually accepted by the agnostic right away, but the really interesting development is that a few years into recovery many of the non-believers develop a strong belief in God.

Developing insight

'To thine own self be true', is an old expression, but in the area of addiction it's a very important one. Early on in initial treatment sessions I urge the clients to get really honest with themselves. The client may be suffering from addiction/alcoholism or they may be a scared spouse trying to come to terms with the blight that alcoholism brings to the family. An important aspect of recovery is for the client to possess or develop good insight, the ability to look inside oneself with scrupulous honesty. (I remind you here that insight is rarely present in the mind of an active alcoholic). To help develop insight here are some questions designed to focus your mind on the problem.

- Deep down am I concerned at my drinking? ✓
- Is my attitude to alcohol different to other people?
- Has more than one person suggested I have a problem?
- Do I get irritated when people talk to me about my drinking? ✓
- Do I make deals (never kept) about trying to 'manage' my drinking? ✓
- Has anyone ever suggested I try AA?
- Can I always justify the extent of my drinking?
- Have I ever not remembered part of the previous night's drinking? (blackout) ✓
- If I have more than three drinks do I find it very hard to stop? ✓
- Have I ever failed a breathalyser test or crashed a car under the influence of drink?
- Do our family finances ever suffer as a result of my drinking?
- Can I get verbally abusive with drink taken?
- Have I ever got into a fight/row while drunk? ✓
- Has my wife/husband ever threatened to leave me over my drinking?
- Have I under-performed at work as a result of hangovers? ✓

- Has my drinking been commented upon by employers/colleagues?
- Is there part of me that wishes alcohol had never been invented? ✓
- Do I try to blame other people/events, for my drinking? ✓   9

For The Spouse:

- Do I ignore what my partner's drinking is doing to him/herself or the family?
- Do I get defensive when someone comments on my partner's drinking/behaviour?
- Do I tell lies on their behalf to family/friends/ employers?
- Do I partly blame myself for their drinking?
- Do I sometimes drink too much to kill the pain and despair?
- Do I try and 'fix' them by nagging and telling them how to cut down?
- Do I believe them every time they say they plan to change?
- Am I scared to ask for help?
- Am I secretly ashamed about what is happening within the family?

- Have I ever threatened to leave him/her?

There is no totting up answers for this one. Rather, it's designed to make you look into yourself. If you have a problem with alcohol and if you're honest enough you'll find much of the content uncomfortable reading. If your spouse has an alcohol problem and you're trying to ignore it, then you too will find this questionnaire a tad uncomfortable. There is plenty of help out there for both parties. Have courage, get honest and ask for help.

There can never be a clear and concise definition of alcoholism but lets try and keep this bit really simple. If you answered 'yes' to four or more of the first set of questions, then the odds are you're probably alcoholic. The more 'yes' answers you tick indicates the extent of the problem. For the spouse, if you answer 'yes' to three or more of the questions, you have, or are developing, co-dependency. You both need to get help.

Yes, it does take courage

Although we can accept that alcoholism is an illness, it is the responsibility of the alcoholic themselves to do something about it. In fact they are the only ones who can work towards their own recovery. No one actually recovers from alcoholism, we are all always in recovery. It's an ongoing daily task.

That horrible word, abstinence, is the foundation upon which recovery is based but as I said earlier, putting down the drink is the easy bit, learning to cope with the ups and downs of life without it, is the hard part. *Without a clear recovery programme the newly dry and, 'I can do it by myself' alcoholic will experience only the pain of white knuckle sobriety. They will become angry and resentful of 'normal' drinkers, be impossible to live with and usually end up drinking again, just to take away their inner demons.*

So, what is all this recovery stuff about? I'll explain it by going back to the word sobriety. Sobriety is to recovery, what golf is to tennis. Golf, you can play by yourself, but not tennis. Recovery is something you can only do through and with other people. It's why I still go to AA meetings. I need to listen to other alcoholics at various stages of recovery and remind myself I'm one of them, and I will be till the day I die.

Deep down most alcoholics know they have a serious problem but the thought of life without the crutch of alcohol terrifies them. Insight usually starts when they have run out of excuses, to make to themselves and others. Scary thoughts like, 'it's over', start to penetrate the fog of early morning hangovers. Slowly, they begin to realise they are sick of lying, denying, fighting, ducking and dodging reality. They are simply sick of being sick. If they're lucky then one day they'll say to themselves, 'I can't do this anymore, I need help'. That moment of insight, of honesty, can be the first step on the road to recovery. If you find you are identifying with this then I urge you to ask for help now. Phone AA (01–453 8998) or a treatment centre or an addiction counsellor. Keep repeating, like a mantra, 'I'm powerless over alcohol, I can't stop drinking and I need help'. Go and repeat it in the front of a mirror. Believe in the words, feel their meaning and seek out help. It can be the beginning of a new and joyous way of living.

I'm not saying your journey will be an easy one but if you put as much energy into your recovery as you did into your drinking you will get well and it will have been worth it!

Courage is defined as the ability to do something that frightens you – having strength in the face of pain and having belief despite experiencing fear. If you have an alcohol problem then I suggest you read the above again, maybe three times over. For an alcoholic, stopping drinking one day at a time will be the toughest challenge ever faced. It takes real courage to embark on the journey of recovery. Yes it's difficult but hundreds of thousands of alcoholics get sober around the world every year. *They don't just put down the drink; they learn to cope with life without relying on drink.*

The prospect of facing a life without alcohol is a truly frightening prospect for the alcoholic. That's where courage comes in. Courage is what's needed when faced with your own demons and fears, the defining moment that all recovering alcoholics face. That scared trembling voice in your soul that says, *'I can't go on with this kind of life. I'm sick of being sick. I'm ashamed of what I have become. I'll do anything to stop drinking and stay stopped.'* That moment my friends, is usually a very lonely and frightening one. It's the moment to ask God (if you believe) to give you the courage and strength to ask for help. Recovery is perplexing at the beginning. You need courage in order to actually surrender to the process and you need to admit to yourself and others that you are powerless over the addiction. You simply cannot win this battle alone. You need help. It takes great courage to listen to what our loved ones tell us: *'Darling, I've been putting off saying this, but your drinking is creating a huge problem in our marriage and family, you must now get help'*. It takes courage for a spouse to say this and it takes courage for the alcoholic to hear and accept what's being said.

These layers of courage are needed early on. It takes real guts to pick up the phone and ask for help. Calling a treatment centre, AA or an addiction therapist takes courage. But I promise you that's the worst bit over. At each of the above you'll be met with understanding, non-judgmental love and support. People in this line of work remember what it was like for them in their early days. (Many people who work in alcohol counselling are recovering alcoholics). I can still vividly remember the most dreaded words in the English language: 'My name is Paul and I'm an alcoholic'. I said that at my first AA meeting in London. Since then I've said it many times at hundreds of AA meetings all over the world. Today I don't need courage to say it. It's a simple fact, a badge of honour. Today I'm a recovering alcoholic and it's a long time since I've needed a drink. The courage of my early days has brought wonderful rewards for me. Today I have peace and contentment in my life, I have a loving relationship with someone who has never seen me taking a drink. Today I no longer need to drink. I don't need alcohol to carry me through life. If you want this in your life then call upon all your inner courage, pick up the phone and ask for help.

Many of my clients report with surprise that in early recovery, the ordinary things in life become special, e.g. working in the garden, going for a long country walk or just playing with the kids. To those in early recovery, I suggest you don't try and take on too much too soon. In most cases there are three special areas that will need your energy and attention.

- Rebuilding relationships with the family. This will take time so don't expect miracles early on.
- Work – if you still have a job. If you don't, start looking.
- Regular and frequent attendance at AA. In early recovery you should be getting to at least three meetings per week. After all, is three hours a week asking too much in exchange for strengthened sobriety?

Chapter 8

FOR THE FAMILY OF THE ALCOHOLIC

If you listen to any GP talk about alcoholism you'll find that they tend not to have too much sympathy for the alcoholic. Instead their sympathy usually goes to the family of the drinker. While the active alcoholic blunders destructively through life, it's the family that have to cope with the resulting mayhem. No wonder alcoholism is called the family illness. Indeed, it's the family who frequently emerge with the most emotional damage. Following is a typical morning after speech from an alcoholic. 'Yes I do remember very clearly what happened last night and I don't understand why you're always exaggerating. I was perfectly alright. Why can't you have a little fun at parties and loosen up a bit?' This could be from a husband who had spilled drinks, fallen over furniture and insulted the hostess the previous night. Can you imagine what it's like living with someone like that? 'What you're saying just didn't happen like that,' he might continue. In these circumstances a spouse might begin to doubt her sanity and think she is the one going crazy, not him. It's only natural that she starts to ask herself how she can love such a liar and a drunk. *Not only does the alcoholic deny wrongdoing, they usually twist things so their spouse ends up feeling it's somehow their fault.*

Here's another example of how the spouse of an alcoholic gets twisted up in further emotional turmoil. The alcoholic disgraces himself at a family party. His wife is furious at his drunken behaviour and won't talk to him for three days. He then, to get out of trouble, gives a grovelling apology and 'behaves' for the next week. She feels guilty at being so tough on him and forgives him. A few days later he goes on another bender and causes even more trouble. The wife is furious with him again, but she is also furious with herself for forgiving him the previous week. As this cycle goes on repeating itself you can imagine how the spouse ends up losing all belief in her own values. Put simply, the family want to support the drinker but his addictive and alcoholic personality will ensure he continues to let himself and the family down. Eventually, the family usually distances themselves from the alcoholic and his destructive behaviour. But even that won't work because there is no one better at playing the guilt card than an alcoholic. ('You've all abandoned me, what hope do I have?') At this point the family needs to stick together and, as AL-ANON says, 'detach with love'.

Children are particularly vulnerable in an alcoholic home. One minute they are being smothered with guilt-fuelled love, the next they are being emotionally bullied. Children in this situation simply never know where they stand. Wild mood swings of an alcoholic parent leave the children confused and anxious.

Angry & full of self-pity
– that's the active alcoholic

Anger, self-pity, hostility, fear, defiance, phoniness, arrogance, superiority … these feelings and attitudes are what that family of the alcoholic has to put with every day. The family gradually realises that the person they once knew and loved has totally changed and has withdrawn emotionally from the family. The alcoholic withdraws by hiding behind one or all of the above feelings and attitudes. Why does the alcoholic do this? I have described how alcoholics end up secretly loathing themselves and their behaviour. In order to protect themselves from this self-loathing they build defences. They shut down their emotions. They become unable to give or accept love, joy, gratitude and affection.

By this point, the family is suffering both when the alcoholic is drunk and when they are sober and at times they don't know which they prefer. So, how does the family cope with this turmoil? The two principle feelings common to all families of active alcoholics are fear and shame. Fear for the future and fear of the unknown, as well as confusion over the unpredictable behaviour of the alcoholic and their broken promises, adds to the emotional mayhem in the home. Frequently, spouses blame themselves for their partners drinking and go on to become care-giver to the alcoholic. What can the family do to survive? Please read the next bit carefully. It's rather blunt and even scary but it's a crucial step to recovery for the family.

Accept that nothing you do or say will stop an alcoholic from drinking if that's what they want to do. You are powerless over their drinking. The family need to detach themselves (with love) from the alcoholic. They must not attempt to take responsibility for the alcoholic's behaviour or recovery.

Some guidelines for the family:

- AL-ANON is a wonderful self-help group for families of alcoholics.
- Stop covering up and making excuses for the alcoholic (to employers, children, etc).
- Stop trying to hide alcohol and stop pouring it down the sink, etc.
- Never, ever drink with the alcoholic.
- Offer loving support for their recovery but not responsibility.
- Never discuss their behaviour with them when they have been drinking.
- Together with the family, try and move on with your life. Hopefully, given time, the alcoholic will follow.
- Most importantly – stop feeling guilty.
- Never lose hope. I have seen many so-called hopeless cases get sober and rebuild their lives. Hundreds of thousands of alcoholics each year, around the world recover from talcoholism. Most of those who succeed do so by joining AA.

Accept that you are powerless over another's drinking

Many years ago professionals in the field of addiction noted specific behaviour patterns among families of alcoholics. They described this behaviour as co-dependency. Personally, I don't like or fully understand the word but I do understand the behaviour the word represents. Co-dependency usually refers to a family member who has been sucked into a way of behaving around the alcoholic. This pattern is damaging to them, and in reality is doing nothing constructive for the alcoholic. Put simply, co-dependents become caretakers and enablers.

Co-dependents tend not to just look after alcoholic's needs, they anticipate them. They take the view, 'Your problem is my problem', and when eventually their attempts to rescue the alcoholic fail, they become bitter, angry and end up feeling worthless. Later this acute sense of failure can explode into destructive anger, designed to punish rather than heal: e.g. 'we're selling your car, you drunk, we just can't trust you'. You can guess the all too predictable response from the alcoholic to that!

Only with help themselves do they come to accept the difference between being there for a loved one and trying to save them. Ironically co-dependents sometimes turn to mood altering substances to alleviate their own pain.

In previous chapters I have written about the often imperceptible slide into full-blown alcoholism for the drinker. A very similar situation exists for the co-dependent spouse. No, I'm not saying they end up drinking. Rather, they end up facilitating or enabling the drinker. I have heard horror stories of wives in particular, locked into co-dependency. Some years ago a lady told me how late one night she spent a frantic hour trying to find a late opening off-licence. Her husband was going crazy at home because she had inadvertently forgotten to replace a near empty bottle of whiskey. Apparently it was one of her jobs to always ensure that the whiskey never ran out. Mind you, it was he who consumed most of the bottle each night but God help her if it wasn't replaced daily. Not that he would admit to having a drink problem, it was just that he needed, 'a couple of drinks' to unwind and alleviate of the stress from his job (which in reality was a rather mundane management position). This husband would fall into a drunken stupor on the sofa and eventually stagger to the bedroom at around 4 a.m. In the morning, his wife would lay his clothes out for the day and bring him breakfast in bed. She explained that she developed this ritual to keep him away from the children first thing in the morning. If the 'bear with the sore head' came in contact with them, they inevitably left for school in tears.

Years later, that same lady looked back at her actions with a sense of disbelief. By then she had demanded, and got, a judicial separation. She explained with the benefit of hindsight that she could see how she was persuaded to mind him, to help relieve the stress of everyday living and protect him from the general ups and downs of family life. In the process, though, she had lost all respect for herself and her needs. Nothing was too much trouble if it meant making his life even slightly smoother. Her housekeeping budget, always tight, was made almost impossible by having to fund his whiskey supply. This woman's story indicates just how out of touch with reality the spouse/partner of the active alcoholic can be and it's why getting help is so important for the spouse. If the alcoholic starts a recovery programme and gets sober, it's crucial that the co-dependent spouse gets similar help. The spouse needs to learn to let go and stop trying to protect and fix the alcoholic. They both need to accept the extent of their individual problem.

The most basic emotional need we have as humans is to love and be loved. If we love too much and at the expense of our own needs we run the risk of draining ourselves of emotional energy. Also, we need to remember that the active alcoholic will always love alcohol above anyone or anything, family included. Is it any wonder that co-dependents, tragically, become addicted to pain and suffering in much the same way as alcoholics do to booze?

It is very important that the spouse, as well as the alcoholic, receives treatment. I regularly hear, 'why do I need help? I'm not the alcoholic'. The harsh fact is however, the entire family is affected by the illness of alcoholism. The spouse in particular never escapes unscathed and it's for that reason that it's usually suggested they attend counselling or after-care, especially if the alcoholic has been in a treatment centre, or AA. Getting back in touch with your feelings is really important. Sharing how you really feel after all you've gone through is quite often the foundation for rebuilding a relationship torn asunder by alcohol.

For the family of the active alcoholic acceptance is a key word. *You need to accept that you are powerless over another's drinking* and accept that if the alcoholic in your life wants to drink, no power on earth will stop him or her. It is crucial for your own wellbeing that *you accept that you need to start taking care of yourself.* You may yearn for inner peace and calm but you'll never attain it if you are determined to control the uncontrollable drinking of another. Finally, you must accept that you can't do this without help.

How can the spouse/partner of an active alcoholic intervene in the most constructive manner? First, let's look at a few inadvisable tactics. The one thing you do not offer an active alcoholic is sympathy – all that does is reduce their anxiety, possibly delaying the point when they seek help. Angry confrontations are also not helpful. Deep down alcoholics know they are in trouble so if you 'punish' them it has a negative effect. If a spouse flies into an angry frustrated rage and screams, 'You'd better stop drinking or I'm out of here!', it won't work. The alcoholic merely slips into deep self-pity and angry resentment and then justifies his behaviour. 'With such a narky wife wouldn't anyone drink?' This also strengthens the alcoholics defence system.

But, if you start working on yourself, you'll begin to get in touch with some deeply repressed feelings and begin to think, 'It's not my fault. I refuse to accept responsibility for his addictive behaviour. I refuse to feel guilty!' When you get to that place it's a truly liberating experience.

I ask you to keep in mind two simple words – step back. Step back from minding, protecting and lying for them to family, friends, employers, etc. The only way an active alcoholic will take a long, hard, honest look at themselves is when they have nowhere else to turn and no place to hide.

I'm not suggesting you tolerate unacceptable behaviour – do not – ever! What I am saying though is try to step back emotionally from what is going on. Some people may feel they have no choice but to leave the relationship and you may have to, but, for your peace of mind, give it your best effort before that final step.

What kind of intervention is appropriate? Keep it simple – try to sit and talk. (Not when they are drinking.) If they won't listen write them a letter. Keep it simple and no emotional 'dumping' (e.g. 'You realise that your drinking is going to kill your mother.') Make a list of ten very specific unacceptable things they have done as a result of drinking. Stress to them that you're doing this because you love them and want to save your relationship. Explain that you are no longer prepared to continue with things the way they are and that if they refuse to accept that they have a serious problem and get help for it, then you are not prepared to remain in the relationship. It sounds cruel but it's not. It's called tough love and it's the only kind of love that works for active alcoholics.

I recently read an interesting definition for whether you have a booze problem: *'If drink is more important to you than the problems it causes – then you have a very serious drink problem'*. To put it bluntly, if you answered yes to the above, you are probably alcoholic. It is the very broadness of this definition that makes it so accurate. It's not how much you drink, it's your attitude towards drinking that is the real difference between 'civilians' (normal drinkers) and alcoholics. I have heard so many alcoholics in full-blown denial insist they have a God-given right to drink if they want to and, 'What's wrong with a man having a few pints?' The simple answer is yes, you do have the right to drink if you want to but if your drinking is creating problems in your home life, at work, financially or health-wise, and you continue to drink, then you are alcoholic. Even so, you have the power to continue drinking and the power to destroy your life and that of your family, but it's also their right to eventually say, 'We can't handle your drinking anymore and if you don't get help and stop, we want you to leave the home.' And believe me, this is a situation occuring with increasing frequency in Ireland today.

Elsewhere in this book I write about an alcoholic's need for courage, but I often think that the person who needs the most courage is the spouse/partner of the alcoholic. Unlike the drinker, whose senses are mostly numbed with booze, the spouse has to make tough decisions stone cold sober. It takes real courage to sit a loved one down and tell them that they have a drink problem and need help. It takes even more courage to add that if they don't stop drinking or get help then the relationship may have to end. For most alcoholics it's this kind of ultimatum that's required to put a small hole in the wall of denial that they have so carefully constructed around them.

The principle aspect that co-dependents share with alcoholics is that they are both out of touch with reality. The co-dependent spouse is outwardly in denial of the problem, meaning they cover up the drinking problem to other family members, friends, employers, etc. Inwardly of course, they are traumatised by what's going on. When I work with couples in this situation I try to explain that alcoholism is a progressive illness that never 'plateaus', it always gets worse and worse, sometimes slowly but often rapidly. It won't go away!

If you or your loved ones have even the beginnings of a problem with booze, ask for help before it gets worse. If you got an early cancer warning, you'd do something very quickly wouldn't you? This is no different!

Some questions for the spouse of the alcoholic

Earlier in the book I gave a diagnostic questionnaire; the following is another, but this one is designed to be completed by the spouse of the drinker.

- Is he/she drinking more now than say, a year ago?
- Do they forget things they do or say when drinking?
- Are you worried about their drinking?
- Have they promised to stop but failed to do so?
- Do they get angry/irritable when you talk to them about their drinking?
- Have you ever lied to cover up for their drinking?
- Have you ever been embarrassed by their drinking?

- Do they usually have an excuse for their drinking?
- Do they try and convince you that it's you who has a problem?
- Have you ever 'called in sick' on their behalf due to their drinking?
- Does their behaviour change for the worse with drink?
- Have they ever driven a car while drunk?
- Have they ever crashed a car under the influence of alcohol?
- Have they ever expressed remorse to you about their drinking?
- Have you ever threatened to leave them over their drinking?
- Has anyone else ever suggested they have a drink problem?
- Have they ever lost their licence for drunk driving?
- Have you ever found alcohol hidden in the house?
- Does the person have low self-esteem?
- Do your children ever comment on the drinking?
- Is their drinking affecting what was once a loving relationship?

If the answer to any three of the above is yes then there is a very good chance they have a problem. If you answered yes to five or more, then the person almost definitely has a very serious alcohol problem and needs urgent help. If a drinker continues to drink despite the fact that it is clearly affecting the relationship, then it almost certainly indicates a level of alcoholism. It may not be what you want to hear but it demonstrates that they are choosing alcohol ahead of their family.

Are you slipping into co-dependency?

The following questionnaire might help clarify the extent of the problem facing the family and determine whether you should seek help.

- Do you worry about a family member's drinking?
- Is their drinking causing financial problems?
- Do you feel they love alcohol more than you?
- Do you ever lie to cover up their drinking?
- Have you threatened to leave them over their drinking?
- Do you secretly try and smell their breath?
- Are family meals delayed by the drinker?

- Do you search the home for hidden alcohol?
- Do you feel guilty about trying to control the drinker?
- Does their drinking make you nervous when out socially?
- Do you ever take your frustration out on others?
- Have you ever behaved inappropriately out of frustration with their drinking?
- Are you putting on a brave face for outsiders – but secretly ashamed of what's happening at home?
- Do you feel no one understands your problem?
- Do you ever 'water down' their alcohol or pour them small measures?
- Do you sometimes think it's partly your fault they drink so much?
- Do you 'tip-toe' around them to avoid setting them off drinking?

If you answer yes to three or more of the above it's likely you have a problem that AL-ANON could help you with.

When I make this suggestion to clients, a frequent response I hear is, 'But I'm not the alcoholic – why do I need to go for help?' Well, firstly, you don't have to go, but it will most certainly help you to understand the concept of alcoholism being a family illness. In AL-ANON you will meet kind, caring people who have been through what you may be going through now. They will share with you how their family survived the ravages of alcoholism and co-dependency. There are AL-ANON meetings all over the country. If you call 01–873 2699 they will tell you where your nearest group meets.

What your children really think

Dear Daddy

I hate when you go out to the pub and come home drunk. You do this lots. You are always very cross with everyone when you come home and you make Mummy cry a lot. Next morning we have not to make any noise because Mummy says your head hurts and you are sick. When I was little you were a nice Daddy, but now you are a very, very bold Daddy. I would like my nice Daddy to come back to us and that would stop Mummy crying.

A client recently showed me this letter from her eight-year-old daughter to her alcoholic father. I asked her permission to use it in this book because I thought it one of the most heart-rending cries for help I have ever seen. Raw emotion and fear leaps off the page – anger too.

The daughter (let's call her Mary) knew exactly what was going so wrong for her family because, like all children, she has almost frightening intuition. Her father is clearly an alcoholic bully and those little eyes and ears miss nothing. Mary is unusual for an eight year old though because she has great courage and she chose to do something about her father's drinking. Most children don't. They withdraw into their own little world and suffer the fear and confusion in silence. They too get sucked into the world of family secrecy and shame, e.g. 'Don't tell Granny that Daddy makes Mummy cry a lot'. Here's a thought for those of you with an alcohol problem: imagine, if you dare, the kind of letter your child would write to you if they could...

Adult children of alcoholics

A high percentage of alcoholics grew up in a family where one of the parents was an alcoholic. These early years have a long-lasting impact on the children and many develop the illness of alcoholism themselves, mainly due to inherited genes. Others develop a passionate fear and hatred of alcohol. Here are some questions to ask yourself that may help you reflect on where you are and how you arrived there.

- Do you regularly put the needs of others ahead of your own?
- Are you afraid to ask for your own needs to be met?
- Are you a people pleaser?
- Do you regularly try and fix people and their problems?
- Are you easily intimidated by people?
- Do you find yourself sometimes resenting that you have been sucked into doing something for someone?
- Do you have trouble saying no to people?
- Do you go along with people and their views rather than put your own beliefs forward?
- Do you lack confidence in yourself?
- Do you sometimes like to be invisible in situations?
- Are you in a relationship with an alcoholic?

There is no scoring for this questionnaire but it does serve to focus your mind on why you are the way you are. How we are as adults, spouses and parents is directly linked to how we were treated as children.

A simple example; if, as a child we were forced to take on responsibility for minding the family due to one parent's alcoholism, then guess what — we maintain that pattern in later life.

It's why adult children of alcoholics frequently end up marrying alcoholics. In their own way they become addicted to minding and caring.

So what are YOU going to do when they stop drinking?

I have written in chapter 10 about the vacuum created in the alcoholic's life when they stop drinking. Now I want to discuss a similar vacuum that's created in the life of the spouse of the alcoholic.

Let's profile a typical marriage that's been affected by alcohol. A couple are married fifteen to twenty years, have two or three children between the ages of eight and fifteen. The husband is the alcoholic and the wife is co-dependent. His slide into chronic alcoholism was probably relatively slow for the first eight years but will have sped up considerably in latter years. As his drinking started to cause problems, first in his own life then in that of his family, a very predictable dynamic will have started to develop. His levels of denial will have dramatically increased and he will begin to say things like, 'It's not me who has the problem, it's you'. The wife will also slip into denial and for years she will keep the extent of his problem a secret from employers, friends, relatives, even their children. It will have become her shameful family secret. She will have continued to believe him every time he promised to stop drinking and sort his life out. Gradually she will have become his caretaker. She will have become a mother figure rather than wife or lover. She covers up the extent of his drinking, tells lies on his behalf and juggles increasingly tight family finances. She will be keeping the show on the road. In reality she will have become an enabler.

Usually, as a result of some catastrophic rock bottom, the alcoholic seeks help and starts to get well. Eventually he stops drinking, starts going to AA and gets his life together. Suddenly all the wife's prayers are answered – her husband is sober. She has dreamed of the relief this will bring to her and the family for years, so why then is she frequently still on edge? For years her main purpose and role in life was minding her husband and his drinking. Suddenly, her role has vanished. Her recovering husband no longer needs her to mind and mother him. He now wants her back as a loving wife. It's no wonder she's feeling confused about her role and identity. She often finds herself angry and resentful over her redefined role in the family.

Like the recovering alcoholic, she also needs to draw up a new life plan. She needs to come to terms with her new freedom. She needs to fill the time she used to spend worrying and caretaking, by learning to start caring for her own needs. She needs to fill her mind and day with a fresh new way of looking at life.

I want to stress that AL-ANON can still play an important part in her life, even though her husband isn't drinking. Living with a recovering alcoholic can be very rewarding but still challenging!

The alcoholic will need to continue going to AA regardless of how long they have been sober. I believe the spouse should stay with AL-ANON as well if, for no other reason than they will hear from others how they coped with their spouses on-going sobriety. That's not always as easy as it sounds!

Chapter 9

THE JOURNEY TO RECOVERY

Relapse is when an alcoholic stops drinking for a period of time, (it can be weeks, months or years) but then returns to a drinking pattern as bad, or worse, than before. We counsellors often meet the drinker for the first time at this stage – the stage when all else has failed.

An experienced addiction counsellor will know that relapse should always be viewed as a learning process rather than a disaster. Relapse happens, usually in the early days, to many alcoholics.

The one thing the recently relapsed alcoholic can be assured of, is that no counsellor will be judgmental about the relapse itself. Handled correctly it can be a great learning experience for the alcoholic and the counsellor.

Understanding the 'triggers' to the relapse are key to future recovery.

The early days of being dry are an extremely stressful period for the recovering alcoholic. The family of the alcoholic often has high hopes and expectations of recovery and this can cause huge anxiety for the alcoholic. The alcoholic worries about what will happen if they drink again, because by this point they have usually received the family 'yellow card', i.e. 'One more drunken incident and you're out.' The inner turmoil in the mind of the recovering alcoholic is often so bad that they take a drink just to cope with the stress of it all. Truly a vicious circle!

A great many studies have been done in the area of relapse. Low self-esteem is a factor identified in many such reports. Alcoholics, for all their bravado and bluff, secretly loathe themselves. In early recovery they can have very negative perceptions of themselves. This lack of belief in themselves can often create a self-fulfilling prophesy of doom, which can lead to an eventual relapse. I referred to this earlier as 'white knuckle sobriety'. It rarely lasts and it's the total opposite to the structured, caring recovery programmes offered by AA, treatment centres and addiction counsellors. Those of us who have tried it this way know only too well the pain that failing the, 'I can do it on my own', approach can cause. We also remember just how naked a newly-dry alcoholic feels – no warm blanket of alcohol to protect them from the harsh wind of life's ups and downs.

Powerful and long lasting healing can be done with an alcoholic who is willing and able to discuss what went wrong prior to the relapse. This learning can provide invaluable lessons as to how the recovering alcoholic needs to change their way of living and relating to others around them. But be warned folks, this cannot be done alone. If you find yourself identifying with the above you need to do one thing right now – ask for help! You have nothing to lose and a lot to gain.

The dangers of complacency

Even for professionals who work in the field of addiction, the learning curve never ends. Many of us are ourselves recovering alcoholics ourselves, which helps us better understand the mind of the addictive personality, a mind that to the rest of the world defies logic. When the alcoholic is drinking they are influenced by alcoholic logic and that, unfortunately, is rarely understood by the rest of the world. This alcoholic's logic, usually whispered into their ear by Jasper, can create all kinds of problems for them if they don't recognise his voice.

Every day you don't take a drink or take a mood-altering substance you get stronger. But, the greatest threat recovering alcoholics face is that every day they get stronger, Jasper tries to slip into their mind one simple feeling that has a powerful, destabilising effect – complacency.

The better we do in recovery the more we are inclined to take our sobriety for granted. Recently, I was talking to a man I have enormous respect for in his recovery. He said that after seventeen years he drank again. I asked him what the trigger was. His answer was simple: 'I just wanted to see if I could drink and control it'. Jasper persuaded him to try one vodka on the way home from work. He drank it no problem and went home. Next night he did the same, no problem. But over ten days he progressed to three drinks per night. A month later he went on a bender and didn't come home for three days.

His distraught wife got a call on the fourth day from the gardai in Mullingar asking her to come and get her husband. Looking back on it now he has no idea what happened to create this disaster, except that he, 'got too complacent.' Instead of a couple AA meetings per week he slipped back to a couple per month. He stopped asking his higher power to help him get through each day without a drink. Complacency can also extend to the partners of recovering alcoholics. A friend of mine was recently at a wedding with his partner of five years. They have a wonderful relationship. He has been sober seven years so she has never seen him drink alcohol. He loved every moment of the wedding, even the dance afterwards. But after the band finished there was a disco with mostly young folk out on the dance floor. Until then it had been a pretty classy wedding with no excessive drinking, but by 1.30 a.m. quite a few of the youngsters were being a tad rowdy and having trouble keeping their balance. He had remained at the disco for the sake of his partner who he knew adored dancing. Suddenly out of the blue he had a total panic attack. It wasn't that he wanted to drink, he just realised he had no business being in a disco where folk were getting drunk around him. The point I'm making is that his partner had become so used to his sobriety she had forgotten that recovering alcoholics do need to, on certain occasions, protect themselves. Put bluntly, we have no business being around people who have had too much to drink. My suggestion to recovering alcoholics is they always have an escape route if social events make them feel a little wobbly.

Will I change as a person when I stop drinking?

I was asked an interesting question by a client recently. He asked, 'My wife is worried that I'll turn into a totally different person when I stop drinking – will I?' As with many questions surrounding addiction there is no simple answer to this. Let's get the hard part of the answer over with first. Alcoholics who simply stop drinking but fail to address the varied aspects of their addictive personality usually become a 'dry drunk' and inevitably drink again. Before they drink again they will be angry, resentful and unhappy; they may not be drinking but frequently their alcoholic thinking and behaviour resurfaces and indeed gets worse. Often our addictive personality encourages us to switch addictions, e.g. gambling, sex, food, etc. In recovery, we need to accept that we once had a deep emotional relationship with an object (drink/drugs) and we are prone to try and replace this addictive relationship, if not with an object then with an event, e.g. shopping.

So, where's the good news? Well, its very simple: for those who get deadly honest with themselves, don't take a drink one day at a time, ask for help and start working through a recovery programme. To quote AA: 'A life beyond your wildest dreams' awaits. It's no exaggeration to say that a process of rebirth takes place. A new freedom awaits you. Yes, you do change, but always for the better. A new person will emerge from the old who is more tolerant, more caring and wiser. You will learn to enjoy the simple pleasures of life, sometimes for the first time ever. When I ask those doing well in recovery what has been the biggest change in their lives, they often give the exact same answer: 'Today I have peace in my life'. Peace of mind can never exist for the active alcoholic, yet it's what many yearn for, deep down.

And finally, the unspoken question – 'Will I ever lose my craving for alcohol?' Many alcoholics do indeed stop drinking and never lose the craving. They are usually the unfortunates who insist on doing it their way, on their own. They won't accept help and they won't work at a programme that's been tried and tested. Today, I can truly say that my craving for alcohol has disappeared. I really do not miss it, either its taste or its effects. Even better, I can live in a world where alcohol is all around. I can enjoy a dinner with my partner and friends and watch without longing as they enjoy their wine. I will say, however, that I'm very uncomfortable around heavy drinkers who talk and behave like idiots. I just won't stay in that kind of company. For most of my illness I was what is called a 'functioning alcoholic' meaning I could continue working successfully and conduct myself in public. But even at this level, I can see that alcohol was the most important thing in my life for a long time. For me to move from that place to where I now feel alcohol is of no interest whatsoever, is a bloody miracle and I mean that literally. In my previous life in advertising I really was quite crazy. My partner today still thinks I'm a bit nuts but if I am it's never as a result of booze. She'll never admit it but I think she's kind of attracted to that nutty aspect of me.

Chapter 10

SO WHAT'S THIS AA THING ALL ABOUT?

Alcoholics Anonymous is a topic which causes fear and misunderstanding amongst some alcoholics. But before I explain why, let me repeat what I said in the introduction: neither I, nor anyone else, may speak on behalf of AA. I am not speaking on their behalf now but rather, am attempting to remove some of the misconceptions that exist in the minds of some people about this wonderful fellowship.

I can identify with these fears from when I was first told that I would need to go to AA meetings on a regular basis. My perception of AA was that it's generally made up of drunken 'down-and-outs'. And yes, there are down-

and-outs in AA, but few of them are ever drunk. Go to an AA meeting and you'll find all walks of human life there – bishops, judges, doctors, lawyers, nuns, rock stars and housewives. The best description of AA is from the preamble read out before every meeting:

'Alcoholics Anonymous is a fellowship of men and women who share their experience, strength and hope with each other that they may solve their common problem and help others to recover from alcoholism. The only requirement for membership is a desire to stop drinking.'

AA has certain core beliefs:

- Alcoholism is a progressive illness, which alcoholics did not choose to get, and they cannot stop their compulsive drinking by themselves. This will have created a totally unmanageable life for the alcoholic.

- In AA meetings one alcoholic talking to another creates an impact that no non-alcoholic can achieve.

- Anonymity is the foundation upon which AA survives.

- No experienced recovering alcoholic would be

heard saying, 'I'm never going to drink again'. In AA meetings you'll only hear, 'I won't take a drink today.'

So what is it that scares people so much about AA? In my practice what I hear are the standard but understandable fears. They were the ones I also had many years ago. What if I'm recognised? Will I be expected to speak? Are they God-freaks? In my case it took a couple of meetings before I was able to say, 'My name is Paul, I'm an alcoholic and I need help because I can't stop drinking'. No one crowded me. All they said was, 'keep coming back'. A few people gave me their telephone numbers and said to call if I wanted to talk with someone. I found, much to my surprise, the people at AA were all very normal, warm and friendly. I was dumbfounded by all the love and support they gave to each other. They also gave me simple practical suggestions: 'Make your recovery the most important thing in your life', 'Keep it simple', 'Go at your recovery with the same energy you went at your drinking', 'Don't take a drink one day at a time'. These sentiments kept me going during the early days of my recovery. Today many of my best friends are in AA and I still go weekly. I need to go to remind myself that I'll always be a recovering alcoholic. The most powerful set of words I have ever heard are said at the end of every AA meeting: 'God grant me the serenity to accept the things I cannot change, the courage to change the things I can, and the wisdom to know the difference.'

AA is not for me, I'm different

I always urge my alcoholic clients to start attending AA on a regular basis. Some start going early on. Others take time to accept that AA is crucial to their long-term recovery.

It's usually only after several attempts at doing it 'my way' that they realise 'my way', doesn't work. It can take months, even years, of slipping and sliding in and out of sobriety before they grudgingly agree to give AA a try. Usually it's with the proviso that, 'It may work for others but I'm different, it won't work for me'. I gently remind them that they have tried every other way to stop drinking and nothing worked. What have you got to lose trying the AA way? It works for millions around the world, so try and give it your best shot. Sometimes the response to that is, 'But I'm coming to you every week, I've stopped drinking a while ago, so why do I need AA?'

The simple answer is that no addiction counsellor can take the place of AA in the long-term.

A common problem for the newcomer to AA is that they tend to compare another's drinking to their own. This leads to the, 'I'm not like them' attitude. It's suggested that newcomers try and identify, rather than compare with other alcoholics. Recently a client who had been to AA a few times reported, 'AA is not for me, I'm not getting anything out of it'. When I enquired further she said, 'Most of the people in AA have had terrible experiences as a result of their drinking. I know I have to stop drinking but nothing really bad happened to me so I have trouble fitting in with them'.

My reply was to say, 'You mean nothing terrible has happened to you yet!'

Much of my work, and that of other addiction counsellors, focuses on trying to help the alcoholic avoid a catastrophic rock bottom. Our challenge is to help the alcoholic develop a brief but true moment of insight. This in turn often manages to put a vital breach in their wall of denial.

Remember, alcoholism is a progressive illness and therefore there is no place for the word 'yet'. Alcoholism never stands still. Keep drinking, even as a mild alcoholic and you are likely to end up a chronic alcoholic! You are no less of an alcoholic just because your world hasn't come crashing down around you – yet. Some have to hit rock bottom before they surrender and ask for help. Others do not let 'yet' interfere – they get honest with themselves before they hit rock bottom and make recovery the most important thing in their life. And that's the only way to do it. They'll know they're getting well when, on entering an AA meeting, they can say to themselves 'I'm an alcoholic and this is where I belong. I'm no different from anyone else here. I'm here because I don't want to drink today'.

I'm not drinking ... what more do you bloody want?

Alcoholics drink when faced with problems/setbacks both real and imagined. They drink to celebrate real or imagined success. They drink because their life is stressful or because 'life is so boring'. You get the picture? The rest of the world gets on with life – without needing to constantly numb itself with alcohol. Textbooks refer to this numbing behaviour as 'mental mismanagement'. You can now see therefore that simply cutting out the alcohol is only part of the challenge. Tackling the mental mismanagement is what takes place in a treatment centre, with a therapist or in AA – it's crucial.

If they do not face up to it, the recovering alcoholic ends up shrouded in angry resentment, which manifests itself in waves of crabby resentments and self-pity. The individual not on a programme tends to overreact to simple frustrations and can be very judgmental and unduly sensitive. They are also hypercritical of others, tense and unpredictable. I can certainly identify with all of that behaviour from my early, 'do it my way', days of sobriety. It is not uncommon for the family to report that the alcoholic was easier to live with when he was drinking.

The above behaviour is often referred to as that of a 'dry drunk' and causes further misery for the family of the recovering alcoholic. If anything negative is said to them, their typical responses might be, 'I'm not drinking am I?' 'That's what you wanted isn't it?' 'What more do you want?'

Unknown to the alcoholic, this thinking and behaviour is steering them straight back into a relapse. They end up taking a drink just to feel normal again. They rationalise their way into taking the odd drink just to, 'gradually get used to being sober' (now there's a classic piece of alcoholic logic). All this will have occurred because the mental and emotional problems of the drinker were not addressed at the beginning of recovery.

At the risk of sounding glib, I would suggest that putting down the drink is the easy bit. Living life without it is the hard bit!

Filling the vacuum left by alcohol

The alcoholic's preoccupation with booze isn't merely confined to the moment of consumption. Recent research in the USA indicated that anticipation accounts for nearly 50 per cent of the enjoyment of alcohol. I regularly hear from clients that they sometimes start thinking about their after-work drink at 11 a.m.!

The anticipation of the drinking session would drift in and out of their thoughts throughout the day. Take into account a modest two hour boozing session and you end up with approximately nine hours a day thinking about or consuming alcohol. One doesn't need to be a genius to figure out that when the alcoholic finally stops drinking this time needs to be filled with thoughts and activities other than booze and how much we miss it.

Yes, putting down the drink is only half the battle. Getting sober for a day isn't too difficult – staying sober on an on-going one day at a time basis is the challenge. For alcoholics the real difficulty is coping with life's ups-and-downs without the crutch of alcohol.

The only way of doing it is to change the way we live, the way we think and the way we interact to people around us. We need to monitor ourselves closely in the early days. Jasper will be playing regular mind games with us, tempting us and trying to rationalise why we 'deserve' a drink.

Going back to filling the vacuum – firstly, too much introspection is really dangerous. Sitting and thinking about your past behaviour only adds to low self-esteem and that's the single biggest cause of relapse for recovering alcoholics. Having too much time on your hands is also dangerous. Getting back to work is important if you have been 'off sick'. Drifting through the day without a plan or schedule also tends to produce the dreaded introspection.

I encourage alcoholics in early recovery to try and draw up a new (but not too ambitious) life plan. Is there a hobby or sport you always intended to learn or start? Do you need to reconnect with your spouse and children? Do you need to take a fresh look at your career?

AA can also stand for Altered Attitude

They say in AA that apart from the letters standing for Alcoholics Anonymous, they also can mean Altered Attitude. I think it a very wise observation. A change of attitude is crucial if the recovering alcoholic is to attain long-term sobriety.

The most important change required is accepting that as active alcoholics we choose to deny reality. For example, it can take many years of experimentation and making deals with ourselves before we accept that every time we try to control our drinking it ends in failure.

No amount of negotiating with Jasper will work, that is simply another part of the denial process. Jasper's conversation, as he sits on our shoulder, may go along the lines of, 'OK so they're all telling you to stop drinking, but isn't that a little extreme? Why not just cut down for a while; get them off your back. Why not tell them you'll never have more than two pints a night midweek and four a night at weekends? Tell them you'll cut out spirits altogether, they can't ask for more than that can they?'

The alcoholic has their own way of behaving when faced with a situation. It can be a good situation or a bad one, but the reaction of the alcoholic is usually similar

– mental escape – get high on alcohol. They crave that feeling of numbing euphoria, that buzz that alcohol brings. They do not want to remain in reality. Alcoholics control their feelings by numbing them. I know that doesn't make a lot of sense to a non-alcoholic, but to the addictive personality it does. It's called Alcoholic Logic.

When I work with alcoholics I'm always watching for a subtle change in their attitude towards their own behaviour. I'm watching for a change in their self-perception. The day they realise that they can no longer control their drinking is the day real progress starts. It's also important they realise that they are the problem, not their marriage, family, job, etc.

Addictive/alcoholic logic is used by the alcoholic to justify their unhealthy relationship with alcohol. It's also used with deadly effect to justify the loss of intimacy in marriage, their financial problems etc. It's only when the alcoholic allows honesty and insight into their life that they begin to see what's happening.

Once the alcoholic buys into the concept that the problem is theirs alone, then they can usually accept that it's up to them to do something about it. The only way they can do something about it is to ask for help. That, for every alcoholic, is definitely a sign of Altered Attitude!

Alcoholic? There's a place you can go and never be criticised

'I know a safe place where you can go and talk about your feelings and about everything that's going wrong with your life. The people there will have been through exactly what you're now going through. They'll give you a lot of support and never ever be judgmental of you'.

Put like that it sounds like the kind of place we could all do with. Believe it or not I'm talking about Alcoholics Anonymous. AA is all of the above and more. As I've said before, the world is a lonely place for those caught up in the illness of alcoholism. It's also very scary. We can see booze gradually destroying our lives and that of our loved ones but we feel helpless to do anything about it. Many alcoholics, when their drinking is at its most out of control, look back with sadness and bewilderment. Did we ever think our lives would end up in such chaos? Our dreams were for a happy and peaceful family life, prosperity and the joy of everyday life.

We'll have tried cutting down, switching our drinks, only drinking at weekends, not drinking at weekends, etc. To our horror, one day, we realise that none of this works; booze now controls us instead of us controlling booze. We end up secretly despising ourselves and as our behaviour gets worse, our loved ones gradually withdraw from us and us from them.

The biggest surprise a newcomer gets at their first AA meeting is just how normal everyone appears to be and how well they are. A nervous newcomer is usually met with the words, 'You're very welcome, every one of us knows exactly how you feel at this moment; we've all been where you are now. Just keep coming back and you'll get well'. The newcomer will then hear others talk about how booze caused so much trouble in their lives. How coming to AA regularly helped them get their lives back in order and, most importantly, helped them stop drinking. They'll hear members talk about their problems in an open and honest manner. The newcomer will start to hear things from others that they can identify with.

I encourage newcomers to say at their first meeting: 'My name is x, I'm scared, I can't stop drinking and I need help'. If you are not up to that, just listen to the group, that's ok too.

For the alcoholic it's not uncommon that no matter where they go they feel they're in trouble – in their home, at work, among friends. They feel people are watching and judging them everywhere. It's good therefore that there is a place they can go several times a week where they know they'll be made welcome, listened to and supported. Alcoholics can talk to each other as no others can. I have been sober a long time but AA is and always will be my spiritual home. It is where my friends are!

Making amends in sobriety

Making amends – that's an expression you hear often in AA and recovery. How and when you go about making amends varies dramatically depending on your relationships and the damage done in the course of your drinking. Before you embark on making amends you need to spend a period of time in reflection. Becoming really honest with yourself is a challenging task. Many of your own self-inflicted wounds need to be allowed to heal. The alcoholic is prone to immense self-pity so too much introspection early on can be damaging.

I frequently meet alcoholics whose spouses have left them as a result of their appalling behaviour around alcohol. Even in early recovery the alcoholic's usual reaction is furious anger and self-pity. 'How could he/she do this to me?' is often the overwhelming emotion. Rarely do I hear in the early days the comment, 'She was right, I don't know how she put up with my behaviour for so long.'

While in denial, alcoholics build up strong resentments against those family members who are trying to point out what is going on for them around alcohol. 'What's wrong with a working man having a few pints?' is an expression I have often heard. The answer is, nothing – providing the same working man is not an alcoholic and has not caused pain, fear and heartache in the marriage. For a great many alcoholics, the mental anguish we have caused our families is the area where most amends need to be made. That is something we need to accept when we finally get the message and stop drinking. But, that's only half the battle. Starting a recovery programme is the other half. Putting down the glass but living a life full of angry, bitter resentment is a recipe for disaster and a great many marriages collapse in such situations. The frequently used line, 'Look I've given up bloody drinking for you, now what more do you want of me?' speaks volumes. It indicates that the drinker's motivation was all wrong. Giving up booze in this frame of mind is definitely not making amends.

The ultimate in making amends is accepting that the hurt you have caused your spouse is so great that they no longer want you in their life. Begging and pleading for another chance, and making a nuisance of yourself, is a far cry from making amends.

I suggest to my clients in early recovery that they sit with their spouse and invite them to tell them in detail how it felt for them. How it really felt. Not the actions of the drunken behaviour, but the anguish, the pain, the fear, and the sense of shame that has brought absolute despair to their life. I urge the recovering alcoholic to sit in total silence and absorb the feelings of their spouse. Do not attempt to close them down by saying things like, 'I know how much I have hurt you.' The truth is we do not know the anguish we have caused; we do not know the feeling of despair we created in the souls of our loved ones. Letting them share this is a crucial part of recovery. It's a big part of making amends!

We have to earn forgiveness

'Forgive and forget' is a common expression. We can forgive but, unless we suffer from severe and permanent amnesia, we cannot forget major life changing behaviour and incidents. We all know how true love needs to be unconditional. Not so forgiveness! I believe that forgiveness needs to be conditional in terms of recovery. Those with an addictive personality and whose lives have been seriously impacted by alcohol, are prone to regularly make grandiose gestures and promises to change. In most cases these gestures and promises are completely empty – designed simply to get them out of trouble. Designed to get the wife, husband, parents, or employer off their back so that they can return to their true love – their addiction.

In the early days when an alcoholic promises to change, it is often because their spouse is willing them do it. The spouse of the alcoholic is prone to being sucked into elaborate plans to help the alcoholic cut back and modify their out-of-control drinking. In desperation the spouse goes along with these promises, but deep in their heart they know it won't work. It's quite simple; no matter what their intentions, without help alcoholics are unable to manage and control their drinking in the long term.

As a result, forgiveness becomes a very important part of both the life of the alcolholic and of their spouse. It's an important part of recovery, to forgive oneself and to be forgiven. But it's something that needs to be earned the hard way. Our loved ones need to see real commitment to recovery. This may mean entering a treatment centre or seeing an addiction counsellor. The absolute minimum should be to start going to AA a couple of times weekly.

I regularly have married couples come to me with severe marital problems. The alcoholic in the relationship will say, 'What more do they want? I've given up the damn drink and they're still angry with me.'

The spouse of the recovering alcoholic will respond, 'Yes he has given up drink but that's all he's done. He's not getting any help, he won't go to AA and he's become a bitter, cranky, very resentful man. His and our life has not got better, it's got worse'.

In this kind of scenario the recovering alcoholic can't understand why everyone has trouble forgiving the past chaos he brought to the family. Earning real forgiveness and gratitude means putting the same energy into recovery that was put into drinking. When we do that we change as people and it's usually for the better. That is when we start to be forgiven and start a new way of living.

'I've stopped drinking but will they ever trust me again?'

Mistrust is something that pervades the family of the alcoholic. The seeds of mistrust are planted early on in the period when alcohol starts to become a problem.

At the beginning, the family are willing themselves to believe the far-fetched explanations for the increasingly bizarre behaviour of the drinker. They want the excuses to be true, even if deep down they all know the excuses don't make sense.

As the drinker gradually starts to lose touch with reality because of booze – so too do the family. Lies become the accepted norm with family members. When daddy comes home in a foul mood and heads straight for a bottle of booze, the oft repeated line is trotted out; 'Daddy has a very stressful and difficult job, he's probably had a really hard day so let's all leave him in peace'. In reality daddy is a functioning alcoholic, and mummy is covering up for him. Naturally, in time, the children realise exactly what's going on and thereafter often mistrust both parents.

The spouse of the alcoholic eventually tires of covering up the dark family secret to the extended family, friends and employers, and although they may well remain co-dependent, their soul becomes infused with anger, bitterness and despair. They lose hope and belief and usually sink into a pool of helplessness. The stream of lies from the drunk over the years will have taken their toll.

The spouse ends up mistrusting anything the drinker says.

So what happens when the alcoholic really does take steps to kick the booze? The husband goes to an addiction counsellor and AA on a weekly basis. He struggles and, for the most part, succeeds in staying away from alcohol – one day at a time. Every so often he relapses, although not as badly as before and afterwards he gets back on his programme, usually full of guilt and regret over what happened. The spouse finds a couple of empty cans in the garden shed now and again. This goes on for a couple of months. Progress in definitely being made but the recovering alcoholic frequently reports that his wife still doesn't trust him and, 'she's always snooping around looking for hidden booze and checking up on me'. I try to explain at this point that we can hardly blame our spouse for being slow to trust us again after so many years of lies and false hopes. I usually stress to my clients that we have to earn the trust of our family all over again. Don't blame them for not believing you, instead just say, 'Judge me by my actions not by my words'. To the spouse I say, look for progress, don't expect miracles.

If a family sees a real effort being made, e.g. not drinking, going to AA and/or an addiction counsellor, then it's probably worth cutting them a little slack. By that I mean putting up with them being a tad edgy and snappy occasionally. After all, the recovering alcoholic who is working a programme needs to know that his hard work is at least being acknowledged.

Our sobriety must never be conditional

I was talking to a man recently who was seven months into early recovery. He was extremely upset at what he perceived as a lack of support from his wife. They had just been on a short break to a European city. It was his first holiday sober, and he was looking forward to seeing the sights and generally mooching around the old city. It didn't exactly go as planned. His wife disappeared shopping and was gone for most of the day. She returned so tired that she wouldn't go out for dinner, choosing instead to eat in a rather down-at-heel grill in the hotel. The next day the wife was back in the shops, for the entire day.

There are several issues here that are of note. Firstly, neither party thought to talk to each other about their expectations for the mini-holiday. Sometimes in the euphoria of early recovery we just presume that certain events/situations will somehow work out but without an open and frank discussion, they rarely do. You must remember that if you get sober after years of drinking, the newly sober person is a very different person both to themselves and their spouse. If the spouse has also worked a programme around co-dependency then they are both going to change, usually for the better. Both partners need to get to know each other again.

I now want to return to the idea of support . The definition of support in the Oxford English Dictionary is, 'bear all or part of the weight'. The person describing the holiday said that he felt he may well drink again if he didn't get more support. This is slipping into serious alcoholic logic. Let me spell out what I mean: Our ongoing sobriety must never be conditional on anyone's support. We get sober for ourselves! Sure, everyone in the family benefits but it's down to us to work on a recovery programme with all the enthusiasm we put into our drinking. This is not to say we can't get encouragement and acknowledgement for the hard work we put into recovery. Just remember though, in our drinking we usually have inflicted terrible hurt and despair on our spouse and they can take a long time to work through those feelings. It's why AL-ANON play such an important role in marriages. If the alcoholic gets well and goes to AA regularly, it's only natural for them to look around and say, 'I'm sober now, let's start enjoying life again'. Their spouse however, is often still thinking at this point, 'I'm happy you're sober and well done, but my mind is still in turmoil. You caused us all such heartbreak and despair, I'm not sure I can ever forgive you. I'm going to try but it's going to take time.'

Finally, the really scary bit is that alcohol often masks serious problems existing in marriage. When one partner stops drinking they may realise the continual rows and serious disagreements were not always because of alcoholism. In sobriety you may well look at your relationship with fresh perspective. Nobody who gets sober does so to be locked into an unhappy relationship.

Chapter 11

RECOVERY IN HOLIDAY SEASONS

The dread of Christmas

'Tis the season to be jolly, fah la la la la ...'

But it's not for everyone. As a therapist I see huge pressure on my clients at Christmas. The commercialisation of Christmas has created unnatural hype and the huge expectation that we should all enter into a state of unrestrained joy and merry making – for the entire month of December. Note the use of the word 'should'. Therapists hate it. We 'should' do this, we 'should' do that – how punitive it sounds. For many, the reality is that this is a sad and lonely time of year. It can bring up memories of happier times, memories of loved ones who have left this world or just left our lives. Those less well-off can end up feeling guilty at not providing enough, guilty at not being able to enter into the world of excessive spending and extravagance. But of all the people my heart goes out to at this time it's those with alcohol problems and their families. Our alcohol-obsessed culture has created a festive mood that glorifies unrestrained and out-of-control drinking. 'Sure it's Christmas, why wouldn't I have a few drinks? Why don't you chill out and enjoy yourself?' How often will spouses hear that between Christmas and the New Year, I wonder?

There's another group of problem drinkers for whom Christmas brings a sense of dread. These are the brave people struggling to confront and beat their addiction. Some are in early recovery; others are nearly ready to start on that journey. For them, Christmas is like an awful sense of the inevitable. They ask themselves how they will ever manage to stay sober over the holidays. I'm not going to say it's easy – it's not! But boy, are the rewards worth it. Many drinkers see sobriety as somehow restrictive and they focus on all the things they can't do. The reverse is actually the case – in sobriety we get a freedom we never before knew. This is the freedom to go anywhere, do anything and never have to rely on a mood altering substance to enjoy it.

Tips for those troubled by alcohol at Christmas:

- Go to AA – their meetings at this time of the year are full of people just like you, desperately trying to get through Christmas sober – one day at a time. Sharing your pain will help everyone share their burden.
- If you're a problem drinker, remember there's no such thing as a hopeless case. Miracles happen everyday – I'm living proof!
- Don't look at this period as a four-week-long temptation. Don't take a drink, one day at a time. Keep it simple.

No matter how bad things get, don't give up hope. When you're ready, reach out and accept help, go to AA and listen. You'll hear remarkable stories of how people, many of whom were in a much worse situation than you, managed to get their life back on track. Some years ago Henry Kissinger was asked what, in his opinion, was the greatest export America gave to the world? He said he believed that the Alcoholics Anonymous organisation was by far the most important thing to ever come out of the United States!

Reflecting on Christmases past

Well that's another Christmas over! For some it will have been happy and calm. For others, it will have been tense and stressful and for other unfortunates it will have been downright awful. But happiness is intermittent and it comes and goes even at Christmas – maybe particularly at Christmas.

Of those alcoholics in early recovery, some will have taken it one day at a time, gone to AA meetings and asked their higher power for help and many will have stayed sober. Yes, I know it will have been a very difficult time but the rewards of facing the New Year sober are worth it. Some people in early recovery will have relapsed and gone back on the booze, either big- time or to a smaller degree. Either way, the result will have been the same: their self worth will have taken a battering, leaving them feeling disgusted by what happened. I really urge these people to go easy on themselves. If you've tried and failed, pick yourself up and try again. Believe me, very few get it the first (or second) time. Most of us have to take several runs at sobriety. The secret is never give up!

When you relapse it's all too easy to adopt the, 'may as well be hung for a sheep as a lamb', mentality. When you feel disgusted with yourself, your addictive personality will start whispering in your ear, 'Go on, have a drink, just one'. But the next morning you definitely will not feel better for it. If you managed to stop drinking but recently drank again, my advice to you is simple: don't ever give up hope. Make not taking one drink, one day at a time, the most important thing in your life.

What about those unfortunates who drank their way through the entire month of December? Even among this group, many will have a sense of growing realisation that they can't go on living the way they are. They are beginning to feel sick of being sick and are wracked with guilt about what they're doing to their loved ones. To these people I say: there is hope. There is help. You can get your life back. You can make this year the year you get sober. It won't be easy but thousands get sober in Ireland every year and maybe now you're finally ready to make the decision to get help. If you believe you have a problem with alcohol I ask you to do the following: go to your bathroom, stand in front of the mirror and say the following: A. Drink is causing problems in my life; B. I'm looking at the problem here, right now, in the mirror; C. I can't stop drinking by myself and I need to ask for help.

Freud was right, even at Christmas

Freud is considered by many to be the founder of psychoanalysis and the study of human behaviour. He divided the personality into three areas. The first is the id, the personality with which we are born. Freud described the id as, 'a seething cauldron of instincts and desires. It has no concept of right or wrong. Its desire is only for pleasure and comfort.' This explains the behaviour of a young infant who seeks pleasure always. In healthy people the instinct and demands of the id are curbed and restrained by conscience or parental influence.

For the alcoholic, or indeed anyone suffering from addiction, the id remains a powerful force in their life. Unfortunately, during the Christmas holidays, the traditional festivities seem to encourage the worst excesses of the id. Self-control and conscience get pushed into the background. The chanted slogan from the id seems to be: 'lighten up everyone, it's Christmas!' This translates as, 'forget all self discipline and responsibility'.

When I was drinking, like most alcoholics I very occasionally got a fleeting moment of insight into my situation. 'What on earth is happening to me? Why can't I stop drinking? Why am I hurting those I love most?' This insight was usually instantly repressed, particularly at Christmas. If the above strikes a chord with you, here's what I suggest: stopping drinking before Christmas will be extremely difficult. If you feel you can do it, by all means do – one day at a time. At the same time please accept that you can't do it by yourself so ask for, and accept, help. If you're sick of being sick, today is the day to plan for your recovery. Regardless of whether you feel ready right now, make a decision that the time has come to stop. Pick a specific date to start you recovery in the not too distant New Year and as it gets closer, keep adding layers of acceptance to your mindset. Accept that your life has come to a point where alcohol is destroying you and everyone you love. Try and look forward to a new life in the coming year. Look forward to a Christmas next year that will be happy and peaceful for both you and your family.

A New Year and new found sobriety

When people come to me before the New Year they share their fears regarding recovery. They ask me how they will ever get through the year without drinking.

'Don't even try', is always my response. 'Just don't take one drink on the 1 January.'

'But what about the other 364 days of the year?' they ask.

I usually advise them, 'Do on the 2 January what you did on the first. Don't take one drink for one day.'

Part of the secret to recovery is keeping it simple. You can't keep it simpler than not taking one drink, one day at a time, can you?

What I'm saying is all of us can manage to do for one day something we think we'd never manage to do for the rest of our lives. It's a very basic concept. It's sometimes hard to grasp in early recovery but it works for millions of recovering alcoholics around the world.

Many people in early recovery have other worries. 'What will people think when they notice I'm not drinking? How will I explain it?' There are a couple of ways to answer this and much depends on the individual's personality. Some people can buy time by claiming they are on medication and can't take alcohol. That usually works but in reality it's only buying time. Where possible, I encourage clients to say that they found drink wasn't suiting them anymore and they've given it up for the moment. There's no need to blurt out anything about drink problems or the 'alcoholic' word. By saying out loud that you intend giving up booze, you are not only putting words to your resolve, you're also hearing the words yourself. It's a very therapeutic exercise. On a more practical level, the mere fact that people know that you're trying to give up booze, acts as a deterrent for your drinking in front of them.

The journey to recovery is always a difficult one and I don't attempt to hide that fact. But recovery brings with it rewards most of us can only dream about. Gone will be the crazy obsession with where you'll get the next drink. You will no longer wake up with a hangover. Instead, you will wake with a clear conscience, knowing that you didn't upset or frighten a loved one. You will know for a fact that there is peace and love in your home again and know that the family no longer has to tiptoe on eggshells around you. At last, you will begin to realise that people are beginning to trust you again. Your loved ones will know that if they ask you to do something, you'll do it.

If they ask you to be somewhere, you'll be there. Small everyday things like this, the ordinary things in life, will become part of a genuinely rewarding new way of living.

The family needs help too

I think of January as 'acceptance' month. It's a time when many problem drinkers and their families say, 'We can't handle this anymore'. The past year and December in particular, will have left chaos, fear and unhappiness in the mind and soul of the drinker and their family. I'm not a great fan of New Year's resolutions, but I do believe the start of the year is an opportunity to take stock of how we handled our behaviour towards ourselves and others in the last twelve months. Certainly for the problem drinker, their out-of-control behaviour will have left them feeling scared and confused.

I see this point in the year as one of rebirth. Nature is gradually coming out of its winter rest and will emerge with energy and vitality. For those who have been hurt and injured by the illness of alcoholism/addiction, what better time to start the healing and recovery process? The excesses of Christmas may in fact bring some small benefit. Right now many drinkers will feel 'sick of being sick', tired of terrible hangovers, and tired of arguments and angry silences from the family. This may be the time to say to yourself, 'there's got to be another way of living.' The families of alcoholics see the drinker as someone totally unconcerned at their own behaviour, but what they can never be expected to see is the inner pain, shame and self-loathing felt by that same alcoholic.

My message to both the family and alcoholic is to seek help now. Shortly, the very earth around us will come alive with wonderful colour and energy. So too can you. The families of alcoholics have in many cases, lived a life of fear, shame and secrecy. Eventually this will spill out into resentment and anger with the world. Alcoholism is called the family illness because it doesn't just affect the drinker, it can eventually ruin the lives of the entire family. I urge these families to call AL-ANON and find one of their meetings near you. At these meetings you'll receive understanding, love and support. You will hear others share the pain and despair they too have experienced. You will hear how they managed to come through the trauma and go on to enjoy a more stable and fulfilling family life.

For the active alcoholic, and indeed the recently

relapsed, I suggest that you take a step back for a moment and with all the honesty you can muster, reflect on the year gone by. Use all the insight you possess. If even a small scared little voice inside you acknowledges that alcohol is causing problems in your life, then please, seize the moment and do something about it. Ask for help, there's plenty of it out there, but you need the courage to accept this help because one thing is certain, you can't do it by yourself. This can be the year you regain control of your life instead of allowing alcohol to control it for you.

Holiday in early recovery

Another hurdle those in recovery will face is the first holiday. Lord, how I dreaded it! Pretending to the family how much fun it will be, but inside quaking with fear. Getting on the plane sober – what a thought! Getting off the plane sober – now there's a real challenge!

For the active alcoholic, a holiday abroad is a licence to give it a real lash. It is not that every night of the holiday will be a disaster, particularly if their family is there; it's the sheer unpredictability of the alcoholic's drinking that causes much of the problem. The alcoholic could be borderline normal for two or three nights but then go on a two-day bender. Waiting for it to happen is what turns the long-suffering spouse into a nervous wreck. In advance of the holiday there will have been the usual promises of, no drinking at lunch, no drinking before 5 p.m., no drinking after dinner, only drinking beer, only drinking wine, never to get drunk, etc. Usually all these deals go up in smoke within the first twenty-four hours. What kind of logic makes us think we can do on holiday what we can't do at home (alcoholic logic perhaps?). Sometimes counsellors hear the old lines, 'It's the stress that makes me drink. That's why I'll be able to drink on holidays – I won't be under any stress. It will be no problem for me'. This behaviour is what AA has defined as insanity – doing the same thing over and over again but expecting a different result each time! Good old alcoholic logic in action.

On the other hand, if you're in early recovery and working a programme, there are some very specific precautions you can take before agreeing to a foreign holiday. First and most importantly, if you really think there is a possibility you'll relapse, do not go. Postpone it until you're a little stronger. If you do feel up to it, choose your travelling companions carefully. For obvious reasons do not travel with heavy drinkers – in fact you may need to change your friends in future. As you build on your sobriety you'll tend to find the company of heavy boozers rather boring so start avoiding them now.

Be sure to check out AA meetings wherever you're staying. There are usually English-speaking ones in most resorts. Explain to your spouse that as it's your first holiday in recovery you'll need to restrict your exposure to alcohol, bars, etc. Most spouses will be only too happy to plan a dry holiday in return for calm and peace. Try to put structure into your days and weeks, not every minute, but enough so as to avoid having too much time on your hands.

Finally relax and enjoy your sobriety – have a good holiday – by now you'll have earned it.

As I walked along a beach early in the morning on holiday recently, I asked myself the question, what's the difference between a holiday for an ordinary moderate drinker and someone in recovery? There's no point in me saying it's just as much fun not drinking as drinking. For those people who can manage their drinking, the combination of holidays and a few relaxing drinks over dinner, is wonderful. I realise now that, for people in early recovery, going out for dinner, can be a bit of an anti-climax. We can feel flat and a little empty inside in the early days of recovery. But I promise you, that too changes. If we work on ourselves, we can get to a point where we enjoy a nice meal and good company. Now, staying sober will never be the same as going out to give it a 'bit of a lash', but there are a lot of plus points to not drinking for the problem drinker: no rows and fights with spouse/family; no staying out till 5 a.m. and blowing half your cash budget for the week in one night; no blackouts; no spending an entire precious day in bed recovering from previous night's drinking; no feeling disgusted with yourself.

The real benefits of sobriety, however, can be summed up in two words, peace and contentment, and that, my friends, is absolutely priceless. Priceless! Peace and contentment is what we recovering alcoholics get our buzz from.

I suggest (never 'tell' an alcoholic what to do, always 'suggest') that in early recovery the alcoholic needs to reassess the way they look at their average day on holiday. 'Normal' people would usually look to dinner with drinks as the highlight of their day. For me however, this meal is no longer a highlight. I find myself getting up early (minus a hangover) having a walk, buying the papers and finding somewhere that serves good coffee. I really enjoy having this time to myself. It's my treat – to me. Later in the day I might return to that same coffee shop for a tasty cappuccino and pastry. What I'm trying to impart is that you need to learn to enjoy things on holiday other than pre-dinner drinks, dinner drinks and post-dinner drinks.

If you have a booze problem then almost certainly, deep down, you're an unhappy person. Remember this – peace and happiness come with a price: sobriety. I for one think that's not a bad deal at all.

Chapter 12

A NATIONAL OBSESSION

Most people are now aware that alcoholism is regarded as a life threatening illness. In the UK, alcohol related deaths have skyrocketed by 20 per cent in five years. I have no doubt the figure for Ireland is even higher. Nearly six million people in the UK are binge drinkers and a further two million are 'chronic alcoholic' drinkers, i.e. it's going to kill them. These figures become even more tragic when you think of the family members affected. Multiply the six million by three family members and you have eighteen million people who are heavily impacted by the illness. Proportionally, Ireland reflects all the above figures. With these kinds of numbers, how could alcoholism be anything other than an illness; an illness that has become an out-of-control epidemic. To again quote Stephen Rowen, Director of the Rutland Centre, 'Ireland is in the grip of a national obsession with alcohol but is in total denial of it'. If you still have any doubts, just cast your mind back to that great day at the K-Club when Europe won the Ryder Cup – a wonderful celebration – but is there any other country in the world that would have needed the same seriously over-the-top accompaniment of alcohol? Is it any wonder that our youth see alcohol as a vital ingredient to any celebration or party?

I know you may throw your eyes up to heaven at the next bit but stay with me. I want to return to the 'illness' word. With every a new client I begin by trying to include the spouse or family members in a session. I explain in detail that alcoholics are not bad people but they have an illness, one they never asked to get. The spouse/relative usually nods in agreement, at least they do during the session, but their thinking later is often different. Probe deep enough with a family member and you'll often get, 'It's not an illness, it is a terrible weakness.' I recall in the early 'slip-slide' days of my recovery, my partner saying to me in complete frustration, 'it's such a bloody cop-out for you lot to explain away your crazy drinking by saying it's an illness – I'm sick of that word!' And you know what? I can fully understand the screaming frustration that the spouse experiences. It's why AL-ANON can be so helpful for the family. Simply talking to other people in a similar situation can be hugely therapeutic. If that doesn't appeal to you, try some counselling sessions, they can help you come to terms with what's happening around you. Acceptance is crucial for both the alcoholic and the spouse/family. The alcoholic needs to accept that they cannot change other people's attitude towards the illness – they can only be responsible for changing themselves. The family needs to accept that they can never stop an alcoholic from drinking – at best they can encourage him or her to get help. Everyone involved must however, learn to nurture and protect themselves.

Today there's a lot of help available but it means putting aside your pride and your fear, and asking for it.

It's not boozy kids, but boozy adults, that are the real problem

In Ireland we have developed a national obsession not just with alcohol, but with abusing alcohol. Young people here (along with those in the UK) are unique in Europe in that they drink to get drunk. I have clients as young as seventeen who boast, 'It's no bother to knock back fifteen pints on a Saturday night'.

While on holiday in Italy recently, I witnessed a totally contrasting lifestyle. Big, busy cafes open till 2 a.m. where young teenagers, older teenagers and adults gathered to relax, drink, talk and even flirt. The young sat side-by-side with adults and over several hours they would drink coffee, wine, beer and water or soft drinks. The teenagers were not served booze, but they did not feel marginalised, as they were included in the relaxed open atmosphere. No one ever got drunk or loud, with one exception. One evening two Irish lads arrived quite drunk. Soon after arriving, their table was laden with empty bottles and the air was filled with loud cursing and foul language. They were swiftly ejected. God, did I feel ashamed to be Irish! It is an accepted belief among psychologists that a great many young drinkers drink to get drunk, not to have a good time. My belief is that the problem is not the boozy kids, but the boozy adults that surround the kids. Parents need to realise that their children learn their life skills and coping skills from them. If kids witness situations where adults seem to only have enjoyable times and 'craic' when excessive alcohol is present, then how can we blame them for adopting the same distorted thinking?

Social commentators regularly ask why something isn't done by our government to address the problem. (Yes, we have a problem with heroin and cocaine, etc. but the real problem in this country is booze.) We are burying our heads in the sand about the problem, and for the politicians it brings the question too close to home. We all know that if they had the will, the government could tackle much of the alcohol related problems. It's worked in many other countries – why not here? It is estimated that one in ten drinkers go on to develop alcoholism, but among today's younger generation this will probably grow to two in ten! Today, 85 per cent of unplanned pregnancies among teenagers under eighteen years old are as a result of alcohol. Two-thirds of all marriage break-ups are a result of alcohol abuse. Two-thirds of road fatalities are alcohol related. One in four psychiatric admissions are alcohol related. Ireland is facing an alcohol epidemic.

Sorry for this gloomy tirade, but as someone who sees daily the carnage that booze is creating, I can't help but shout loud and clear, 'Please, please stop underplaying and normalising the abuse and danger of alcohol!'

If alcohol were discovered today, it would be banned in every country in the world. Alcohol is the principle ingredient of the anti-freeze we put in our cars; for a lot of folk it would be better if it stayed there.

Does alcoholism differ between young drinkers and old?

Recently, the ex-wife of an active alcoholic asked me an interesting question; 'Does the illness of alcoholism differ between young drinkers and old?' I believe that the middle and end of most alcoholics' drinking, tends to follow a similar pattern: a gradual disintegration of values, morals and self-control, leading to a life of total unmanageability. It's the beginning of the journey that tends to vary. Stay with me while I generalise in order to make a few points. As humans we naturally seek happiness and contentment in our lives but happiness, unfortunately, is intermittent. This coming and going of joy is part of life's reality. Those fortunate enough not to have addictive personalities won't enjoy being unhappy, but they cope with it until things improve. Not so the addictive personality. This person will seek to replace 'down' feelings with the 'high' achieved by mood altering substances or events. This addictive behaviour can be observed amongst people young and old. Put simply, alcoholics, be they young drinkers or old, can't handle life's ups and downs without the crutch of booze, drugs or something mood-altering like excessive work, shopping, sex, etc.

The forty-plus generation tend to drink to have a good time and enjoy themselves, only to find, in some cases, they have developed a powerful dependence on alcohol. They would have been disgusted earlier in their lives if they passed out from drink, got sick, got into a fight, or got arrested. Today's young drinkers are quite different. In many cases they drink for one reason: to get blind drunk.. They 'power-drink', often up to thirty units of alcohol per night. They have absolutely no fear of alcohol and no respect for it. It is suspected that of today's young drinkers, two-in-ten will develop alcoholism.

This country is feeling the grip of an alcohol epidemic. We have one of the highest alcohol consumption rates in Europe. The World Health Organisation quotes figures showing that in Ireland 50 per cent of people between nine and eleven years old have cosumed alcohol. They also report a 50 per cent increase in drunkenness in girls between fifteen and sixteen years old. We now know that people who start to drink alcohol before fifteen years are twice as likely to go on to develop alcoholism in later life.

Addiction is the same terrible illness for young and old, although the consequences of the illness are greater for older drinkers with families. The aggressive, go-for-it style of binge drinking among today's youth is merely speeding up the process and journey into full-blown alcoholism. Here's a depressing but factual piece of information, one that confirms that we should all refuse to accept the culture of alcohol that wraps itself around our youth in Ireland: people under twenty-one years old are the only age category who are dying in greater numbers than 100 years ago. Sadly, they think they are indestructible. Visit an A & E ward on a Saturday night and you'll see that they are not! (Apologies to those young folk reading this book who do drink responsibly – I had to generalise to make my point.)

The majority of adults are puzzled and worried by the out-of-control binge drinking of young people. We shouldn't be puzzled. All young people acquire and learn their life skills and behaviour traits from adults. We now know that in Ireland the average adult male 'binges' on six-out-of-ten drinking occasions. With this kind of example being set, how can we act surprised if young drinkers do the same? All research indicates that binge drinking among young male and female drinkers is dramatically on the increase and hospitals are now reporting a huge increase in young women suffering from acute liver failure.

In Ireland alone, one-third of fifteen-to-sixteen year-olds binge drink regularly. In a recent survey published in the *Irish Times* it was reported by GPs that out of 2,290 patients, one in five had an alcohol problem.

Ireland now tops all worldwide charts for alcohol abuse. In a recent survey of nineteen countries our students were shown to drink more than any other country. The same survey showed that 57 per cent of Irish female students were classed as, 'heavy drinkers' – a whopping 20 per cent ahead of the next country in the rankings. Irish women drinkers in general also top the world drinking league. Under the 'all adults' category guess who is number one? Yep, that fair and green land of Ireland.

On this last October Bank Holiday weekend, a total of 459 drivers were charged with drink driving. The papers were full of outrage, government ministers promised that things would change, tougher laws would be introduced. Oh yeah? How often have we heard that claptrap. In this country there is no real political and social pressure to address a problem (alcohol abuse) that is going to decimate future generations. The super-power that is the Vintners Lobby will see to it that no meaningful legislation ever gets through our Dail.

Will we ever see tougher penalties for drink driving? More than likely all we will see is a couple of months added to driving licence suspensions and a few hundred euros in increased fines. What we need to do is accept that anyone getting behind the wheel of an automobile with more than four units (two pints) of alcohol inside them is akin to a drunk wandering though town carrying a loaded shotgun. The only difference being the drunk with a gun is easier to spot.

What is happening in this country is a national scandal. Our alcohol abuse problem is dramatically affecting our physical and emotional wellbeing. If the government ever produced a true picture of what alcohol abuse costs the country in terms of lost work days, accidents, hospital charges and deaths, we would be flabbergasted.

What can be done? Let's just take drink driving, for instance. I guarantee that if the following three measures were introduced, we would significantly cut the level of drink driving:

- Fail a breathalyser test and your car is confiscated. If convicted you NEVER get it back. Just think of the impact of that move alone.
- Each month, place full-page advertisements in national daily papers. Photos and names of all those convicted of drink driving are included in the advertisement. Name and Shame them, they are potential killers and the country has a right to know who they are.
- Be convicted of drink driving twice and you lose your licence for life.

Mind you, like all road safety measures, the above would need a level of policing way ahead of what it is today.

Despite what I've just written, I want to state clearly, I am not anti-booze. I am anti-booze abuse. Anyone who thinks I am extreme in my views should drop into any hospital A&E ward on a Saturday night/Sunday morning. You will see many of our young adults, dead or dying, usually covered in blood, vomit and reeking of alcohol. Visit any graveyard on a Tuesday and witness the weeping relatives burying their sons and daughters. Problem, what problem? We don't have a problem, we just enjoy our jar.

Chapter 13

CREATING AN INTERVENTION PROCESS

The greatest obstacle to recovery from alcohol addiction is the deeply entrenched layer of denial that exists within the alcoholic. Ask any family member and they will detail the reasons and explanations offered by the drinker to justify and explain away their drinking. It's usually summed up by something like, 'My drinking is not a problem. I can stop/cut down if I really want to. I'm just under a bit of stress at the moment and I need a few drinks to help me unwind and get through it'. What the drinker rarely mentions is the behaviour that the drinking creates. Many long-suffering spouses would let the alcoholic quietly drink themselves into oblivion.

It's the out-of-control behaviour that accompanies the booze, which creates the trauma and heartbreak for families.

How can the family break through this level of denial? Earlier on I outlined the possible structure for an intervention process. I'm now going to go into a little more detail and reproduce an actual intervention procedure, which worked. What is the objective of interventions? It's quite simple: our goal is to present a glimpse of reality to someone totally out of touch with reality but, and this is crucial, to do it in a manner that allows the alcoholic to accept what's being said. The secret of a successful intervention is to present the facts to the alcoholic in an objective, factual and unemotional manner. The entire exercise is about making the alcoholic (for even a short period of time) face up to the reality of their problem. Yes, it will be traumatic for everybody, particularly for the alcoholic. If it has any hope of piercing the wall of denial it needs to be almost cataclysmic. The tone taken by the family has to be of loving concern and understanding. Try to put aside concerns you may have about the intervention process being underhand or shady. Remember this: alcoholism is a life threatening illness. If a member of your family had an aggressive form of cancer you wouldn't think twice about pressuring them into seeking help would you? This is no different. This is definitely a situation where the end justifies the means. Keep reminding yourself – alcoholism is the one illness that tells you, you don't have it. The greatest act of love you can offer someone is to somehow, someway, get them to face up to their drink problem.

The natural temptation is to delay forcing the issue with the alcoholic. Some people worry that by confronting the alcoholic they may drive them further into despair and hopelessness. Or they may by now be so exhausted and weary of trying to fix the drinker that they feel, 'What's the point, nothing works anymore, he/she's never going to stop drinking'. If this book does nothing more than instil a sense of hope, and remind you of the need to never give up hope, then it has achieved something. My personal and strongly held view is that there is no such thing as a hopeless case. I'm not saying that you should continue trying to take responsibility for their recovery but I do suggest that even as you step back after the intervention, you never lose hope.

In my work I come across a wide variety of cases where people's lives have been blighted by the illness of alcoholism. Today, there is clear evidence that recovery is much more achievable in situations where the alcoholic has not lost it all, e.g. family, employment, finance and health. The point I'm making is that the sooner the alcoholic's wall of denial is breached, the better their chance of recovery. That's why intervention, painful and traumatic as it may be, is definitely worth the effort.

The final rationalisation you may use to avoid taking action might be, 'Maybe if we just let him go on drinking he'll realise the seriousness of the situation and book himself into a treatment centre?' Elsewhere in this book I discuss the fact that for alcoholics, unprompted insight simply does not exist. Put bluntly, alcoholics cannot see the utter chaos alcohol is bringing to their lives and the lives of others around them.

What is the principal goal of intervention?

Let's be very clear on this: the objective of intervention is not merely to break the wall of denial around the alcoholic. (That's merely the lead-in to the crucial part.) The objective is to get them, there and then, to agree to take specific steps towards recovery. Let me stress that your objective is not to get them to promise to stop drinking there and then. (It's the easiest cop out for the drinker. 'Ok, if that's what you want I'll stop, cut down', etc.) The options you need to spell out are clear, actionable and immediate:

- Enter a treatment centre, or
- Attend an addiction counsellor, or
- Start going to AA regularily

We'll go into more detail about these objectives in the next section of the book.

A question frequently asked by the family at this point is, 'Why do we need a group of people to confront him/her? Why not get one person to have it out with him/her? Those of you who have tried this one-on-one confrontation will know the answer. The explanations, which have been developed over time by the alcoholic, are so strong they render any meaningful discussion useless.

For an alcoholic, facing an unexpected intervention group is their worst nightmare. It's something they never, ever thought would happen. Again, I don't want this planning to sound harsh or cruel, it's not. It just might, however, save the life of the alcoholic and the sanity of those who love them.

I'm now going to describe in detail the 'ideal' intervention. Few can manage to structure it perfectly in terms of who attends but you can adapt and make the best of those concerned persons who are willing and available.

Who should be part of the team?

It can help to have an experienced addiction counsellor spend a couple of hours with the group in the weeks before the intervention, and even better if you can get them to sit in and act as moderator. But, and I stress, this is not vital. Plan it correctly and you can run this yourself.

Often, if you are leading an intervention, you are the spouse or parent of the alcoholic. For arguments sake let's say you are the wife. In total, you are looking for approximately six concerned persons to make up the intervention team. Consider the following:

- The Employer: They can be a powerful player in the session. Naturally, however, you don't want to put his employment at risk but frequently a sharp boss is only too aware of the booze problem. If the employer values your husband as a worker and is a caring and compassionate person, they may well be willing to join the team. Their presence usually ensures that the alcoholic will at least listen to what is being said by everyone. Plus, any ultimatum given by a group that includes his employer is hard to ignore.

- Mother/Father: A proviso here, only include them if they are emotionally and physically strong enough. They will also need to have a good relationship with the alcoholic, even if it has been strained by his drinking and recent behaviour.

- Children: Children can play a huge role in intervention. They should be 9 years of age or older. Yes, I know you fear they will find it too upsetting but make no mistake, these children will have witnessed the slide into alcoholism by their father. They may not say much but they will have taken it all in. An intervention process is often the opportunity for children to voice their anger, fear and disappointment at their drinking parent. The deciding factor as to whether you include children is, can they articulate to their father at least one drunken incident that really upset them? Don't tell them what to say, let them speak from the heart.

- Brothers/Sisters: Again a simple rule here – do they have a half-decent relationship with their alcoholic brother? Do they care for him? Don't invite a sibling that has any kind of addiction problem. The last thing you need is for the alcoholic to turn on his brother or sister and say, 'Who the hell are you to talk about booze, you're pissed every Saturday night'.

- Friends: These may be friends who in the past have said to you or the drinker that they thought his drinking was getting out of control. They may well be friends who have drifted away as a result of the alcoholic's overly enthusiastic levels of consumption and subsequent behaviour.

- Clergy: A very, very strict proviso here – use clergy only if the alcoholic is religious and respects a particular clergyman. If this is the case, by all means include him. Take care to ensure there is no talk of sin, hellfire and damnation, etc.

What is to be communicated?

The secret to a successful intervention is detailed preparation. Bear in mind that an intervention should never degenerate into a family slagging match. You're attacking the illness and the wall of denial not the drinker. Nobody should get personal, e.g., 'You've become a selfish bastard and lousy father'. The people you pick for the process have to learn not to 'lose it' emotionally. Everyone should have a list of three incidents where the drinker did or said something unacceptable as a result of alcohol.

Whoever opens the meeting must stress that this is very painful for everyone. It's not about blame. The intervention is being done out of the profound love and concern everyone present has for the alcoholic. Naturally, you can expect the usual defensive arguments from the alcoholic. That's why it's so vital to have at least one rehearsal. You, the spouse, will have heard them all before, so you can share with the others his likely rationale for the alcohol abuse. (Stress, nagging wife, demanding children, demanding job, etc.) Decide who is to go first, then put a running order on it. I suggest the strongest most articulate person should start off, with the children speaking in the middle. End with someone strong, preferably whoever is running the meeting. Remember, you're not looking for feedback from the alcoholic during the session. At the start of the intervention you ask that they do not interrupt and that they listen to what you all have to say.

It is really important that at the end of the meeting you propose three treatment options. Make sure you've done your homework and that there are immediate plans ready to be put into action. I suggest something along the lines of, 'Your case is packed and your boss is giving you a month sick leave. The treatment centre can take you this afternoon and our health insurance will pay for it'. Another option would be, 'You have an appointment with an alcohol counsellor this afternoon and your friend Harry is going to take you to your first AA meeting at 8 p.m. tonight'.

Be aware that the alcoholic will duck, dodge and do anything to put off a firm decision. Do not accept the, 'I need time to think about it' line. The drinker needs to realise that no one is bluffing at this meeting. If the boss tells him he's in danger of losing his job, he should be ready to fire him. If you threaten to leave him, be ready to do so. If his parents say they don't want to hear from him again unless he gets help, they must tell him as bluntly as they can.

However, there are some situations where an intervention is not recommended: if the person is particularly violent and aggressive, or if they suffer from mental illness or severe depression. (As opposed to the usual alcohol induced depression). Also, never try an intervention when the person is drunk, although, it can be very effective when they're hungover or 'seedy'. The meeting shouldn't drag on. Everything that needs to be said can be said in an hour.

Timing and location of the intervention

Morning is a good time to hold an intervention because usually (but not always) the alcoholic hasn't had their first drink of the day. It will be up to you to concoct a story that will get them home or to someone else's home where they will be unexpectedly confronted with the intervention team. I'm sure it doesn't need saying that the story should not involve a drama such as an accident or very sick family member.

What happens if he walks out?

Yes this does happen sometimes. Don't think of it as a total failure. You can be sure that the drama of the situation will have had a catastrophic impact on him. It may not stop him drinking straight away but it will have had an impact. At the very least it will ruin his enjoyment of booze for a while. For the family, the entire exercise will have flicked on a light switch. There will be no more dark family secrets, it's out in the open now, and that's usually of immense relief to everyone. It also makes taking tough decisions a little easier. If you've been worried about rearing your children in an alcoholic home then this may be the push you needed to ask for a separation. This in turn may be the spark necessary to persuade your partner to get help.

Finally, if he does walk out it's often helpful to ask everyone who was present to write a short letter to him telling him how much they care for him but how worried they are for him. They should include at least one example of his drunken behaviour, which they were going to mention at the meeting. Each letter should conclude in a caring tone but at the same time express in strong words the problems that alcohol is causing, and that he needs to get urgent help.

INTERVENTION SCENARIO

Jack is a middle management executive in a large company. He's also an alcoholic but in complete denial. Liz, his wife, has struggled to cope with the effects of his drinking on the family. He has two children, a son of eleven and a daughter of thirteen. He is awaiting a court case after having been stopped for drink driving. Recently, his boss called his wife regarding his drinking and behaviour at social functions.

Liz has been attending an alcohol counsellor to try to learn more about the illness and they have agreed to put together an intervention process. After talking to family and friends, Liz has persuaded his boss (Jerry), mother, his sister (Helen) and his old friend and best man Mick, to join the intervention team. Finally, his daughter Mary expresses a strong desire to be there, 'If it helps Daddy get well again'. The counsellor agrees to sit in and monitor the session. They have two lengthy rehearsal sessions with everyone present.

Jack visits his mother every Saturday morning (on his way to golf). His mother, after sitting through the first rehearsal, offers her home for the intervention. Her attitude is, 'I don't care if he never talks to me again as long as it helps get him sober'.

THE INTERVENTION

At 11 a.m., Liz, Jack's boss Jerry, his sister Helen, his friend Mick, his daughter Mary, as well as Tony the counsellor and his mother, gather in his mother's lounge. At 11:20 Jack opens the front door to be met by his mother who asks him to step into the lounge.

Jack: 'What the hell are you guys doing here, has something happened?'

Liz: 'Jack, we've all been meeting for the last couple of weeks to talk about how we can help you face up to your drinking problem.'

Jack: 'Jesus, you're some shit-stirrer, you've gone too far this time ...'

Jack stands up to leave

Jerry: 'Please Jack, sit down for a minute and just listen to Tony, he's an alcohol counsellor and he's been working with us.'

Jack: 'I don't need any bloody counsellor, it's you lot that need help, not me.'

Tony: 'Jack, everyone here is very, very concerned about what drink is doing to you ... All we ask for is one hour of your time – just listen to what we have to say. These people are here because they love you. Just take a look at your daughter's face, your mother's face, they're heartbroken and scared about what has happened to you.'

Jack: 'I have to go. I'm due on the first tee in twenty minutes ...'

Jerry: 'I rang the club and told them you won't make it. Jack I'm your boss but I like to think I'm also a friend to you and Liz. We need you to sit back and listen to what's going to be said. If you don't I can't continue propping you up in your position at work.'

Jack: 'You mean you're going to fire me?' (To Liz) 'See what you've done you stupid bitch, you've got me fired.'

Tony: 'Jack, if Jerry was going to fire you he'd have done it long ago. Now will you give me your word that you'll listen to what your family, your friend and your boss have to say to you?'

Jack, by now staring at the floor, nods angrily.

Liz: 'Jack, we've been married for eighteen years, the first ten of which were wonderful. We didn't have much money but we were inseparable. But in the last five years your drinking has gradually gotten out of control. When I took the bottle of gin off the table after dinner last month you slapped me across the face, in front of our children ...'

Jack: 'That was the first time ever and I promise ...'

Liz: 'That's not the point, Jack. You would never have done that if you were sober. You remember going on the plane on holiday with the children last year?'

Jack: 'No, what are you talking about?'

Liz: 'The air hostess refused to serve you more alcohol because you were so drunk, when you started cursing at her the pilot came down and threatened to have you arrested when we landed. Can you imagine how your family felt as we got off the plane with you? We wanted to get on the next flight home and leave you there.'

Mother: 'Jack, do you remember your father's anniversary mass three months ago? It was on a Friday evening. You turned up in the church quite drunk. You had driven there drunk and afterwards you started shouting at Liz and the children when they wouldn't get in the car with a drunk driver. Later when we came back here for tea and sandwiches you stopped in the pub and eventually came back even drunker. I had to ask you to leave and you cursed at me when you were going. Jack, five years ago you would never have behaved like that. You were such a kind son to me but now I'm ashamed of what you're doing to your lovely family.'

Jack is now sitting with his head in his hands.

Mick: 'Jack, you know I love a pint or two after golf. But just think back, in the last year alone I've heard the barman in the golf club refuse to serve you anymore drinks because of how drunk you were. He's had to do it at least three times. You're getting a reputation as the club drunk. Up to a year ago, you, Liz, me and my wife used to go out for dinner. She won't do it anymore; she thinks you've become an obnoxious drunk. Jack, we've known each other since we were 8 years old, you're my best friend and I love you. But I'm telling you here and now I can't and won't be around you anymore if you don't go and get help for your drinking.'

Helen: 'You probably don't know this but when you're drinking at weekends your two children sometimes ring me and ask can they come and stay. Don't you wonder where they are when you're drinking? They either lock themselves in their rooms or come over to me. You remember our New Year's Eve party last year? You got really drunk and started a terrible row with our neighbour. You ended up ruining the night for everyone.'

Mary: 'Daddy, I want you to listen …'

Jack jumps up, 'Stop it, stop it, surely you don't intend dragging a young child into this – it's not fair on her …'

Tony: 'Listen to what your daughter has to say. She asked to be allowed to speak. And it's not fair on her. It's not fair on her to have to put up with a drunken out-of-control father. But she, like everyone here today, is hoping that what is being said will make you realise that you must go and get help for your drinking. She loves you – so please listen to what she has say.'

Mary: 'Daddy, I really do love you but I'm so scared of you when you're drinking. I hate it when you start shouting at Mummy. Last week when you came to the final of a camogie competition that I was playing in, you were drunk and shouting like a mad thing from the sideline. You ended up in a row with other parents who told you to stop swearing. You thought I was substituted, I wasn't. I pretended to be injured just to get off the pitch and away from you because I was so embarrassed. I was ashamed of my own father.'

By now Jack is sitting up with tears streaming down his face. His body is convulsed with sobs and shaking. Thanks to the hard work at the rehearsal, everyone else is just about holding their emotions in check. Jack's mother and daughter have tears in their eyes.

Jerry: 'Jack, up 'till three years ago you were one of the best managers we had. But since then your performance has gone to hell. You miss targets and deadlines. You're hungover at least three mornings every week and I'm getting more and more complaints about how you treat people.'

Jack: 'You never objected to me kicking ass for you
        before …'

Jerry: 'No, I didn't, but you lose all credibility when
        you do it stinking of booze and with bloodshot
        eyes. You've been off work with 'food poisoning'
        and flu fifteen times this year and strangely
        enough food poisoning seems to always strike
        on a Monday. I also know for a fact that you've
        started drinking at lunchtime. Last week a
        client complained to me that you stank of
        booze in a meeting at four in the afternoon.'

Jack: 'So what – he signed the bloody contract didn't
        he?'

Jerry: 'Yes, he did, but he also rang later to say he
        doesn't want you near his business again. That
        client used to respect you. Today he thinks
        you're a drunk. I'm putting it straight to you
        Jack, get help now or your future with us is on
        the line. I want the Jack I used to know back
        with us. You need help and you need it now.'

*By now Jack is staring at everyone with sullen defiance.
Liz walks over and hands him an envelope.*

Jack: 'What's this, more hate-mail?'

Liz: 'No Jack, it's a letter to you from my solicitor. If you don't get help for your drinking I'm leaving you. I'll suspend any action by the solicitor on one condition – that you agree to get help now. If you don't, I promise this time next year you will not be living with me and the children.'

Jack crumbles and starts to sob uncontrollably.

Jack: 'Jesus, Liz, what are you trying to do, destroy me?'

Liz: 'No Jack, despite what you think we are all trying to save your life. Drink is killing you; it's destroying your life and ours. The worst part of all is you think there's nothing wrong.'

The only sound in the room is Jack's sobbing. The atmosphere is highly charged with emotion – pain, fear and love.

Jack: 'Fuck it then. If you want me to stop drinking, I will. Then will you all get off my back?'

Tony: 'No Jack. Today is not simply to get you to agree to stop your drinking. We all know that you've tried that many times and it never works. Jack, you're an alcoholic and you won't be able to stop and stay stopped by yourself.

You've heard some very painful facts from the people in this room, people who love you more than anyone in the world.'

Jack: 'If you don't want me to stop then what the hell do you want me to do?'

Liz: 'There's a bag packed outside and you're booked for a month into a treatment centre. It's all arranged and covered by our heath insurance.'

Jack: 'No way – I can't take a month off work …'

Jerry: 'I've organised that Jack. It'll be worth it to get you back in good shape.'

Mary: 'Please Dad, please go and get well again. We all want you back like the Dad we used to have. We'll come and see you every weekend, I promise.'

Tony: 'Jack, up to now you've lost nothing, but if you don't go and get help today your world is going to disintegrate very quickly. No one can make you get help but if you choose booze ahead of the people in this room, you'll end up losing every one of them. It's decision time Jack.'

Jack gets up, walks over to his wife and puts his arms around her. Tears are pouring down his face.

Jack: 'Liz, I'm so sorry for what I've done to you all. I hope that one day you can forgive me. I'm terrified at what's ahead but yes, I'll do it.'

At this point everyone embraces Jack, tears flow, as does an outpouring of love.

N.B. This intervention took place last year. Jack did a month in the treatment centre and is still sober today. The various names have been changed and permission given to recount this family's experience.

There is hope...

Those of you who have read this book will have done so for a variety of reasons and motivations. Many of you will be concerned family members, worried about the drinking of a loved one. You will have been looking for answers to questions that have plagued you and cost you many sleepless nights. I hope you have now found a new way of dealing with the problems that alcoholism brings to the family. I hope you have learned that if your alcoholic family member really wants to continue drinking then there is very little you can do to stop them. There is, however, much you can do to protect yourself and your family from their behaviour.

If you are one of those fortunate families where the spouse is in recovery and doing well, I hope you have found my suggestions for your recovery helpful.

If you have had to leave someone because of their drinking, take comfort in that by so doing you may have pushed them, for the first time, to take an honest look at their drinking and behaviour. Try not to allow yourself to feel guilty.

If you've read this because you're worried about your own drinking then I salute you. If parts of the book made you feel uncomfortable and made the hairs on the back of your neck stand up, then this could be the first step on your road to recovery. In the course of the book I have suggested there are two levels of acceptance: the first being acceptance that you have a drink problem; the second is equally important and requires you to demonstrate real courage – you need to do something about your problem, you need to ask for help. If you have slipped in and out of recovery or have relapsed after a period of sobriety, don't give up. Get back to AA. If you think some work with a counsellor would help, then get it. Fight for your sobriety. It really is worth it.

At this point I would like to discuss something that has been on my mind while writing the final stages of the book concerning treatment centres and counsellors. If you can afford them they are extremely helpful and supportive, but I want to stress that AA costs nothing, and more alcoholics get sober and stay sober in that fellowship than through all the counselling treatments in the world. One of the mistakes I made was thinking that just because I went to one of the best treatment centres in Europe, I left knowing it all. I thought I didn't need AA or any other recovery programme. You all now know what happened to me. Don't make my mistake, and don't kid yourself that you can do it by yourself.

Finally, never ever think of yourself as a 'no-hoper' – there is no such thing! I am living proof of that. Today my life is in total contrast to the crazy, out-of-control way I once lived. Today my life is good. *If you want what I have today, do what I did, ask for help.*

Paul Campbell is an Addiction Counsellor in Kildare
Email: pcaddiction@hotmail.com
Tel: 086 - 1543772